SAGE SISTERS

SAGE SISTERS

Essential Lessons for African American Women in Ministry

LINDA H. HOLLIES, EDITOR

Foreword by Barbara Blake King

THE PILGRIM PRESS

CLEVELAND

The Pilgrim Press, 700 Prospect Avenue, Cleveland, Ohio 44115-1100
thepilgrimpress.com
© 2007 by Linda H. Hollies

12   11   10   09   08   07   5   4   3   2   1

Library of Congress Cataloging-in-Publication Data

Sage sisters : essential lessons for African American women in ministry / Linda H.
    Hollies, editor; foreword by Barbara Blake King.
        p. cm.
    ISBN-13: 978-0-8298-1764-5
        1. African American women clergy.   2. Women in church work.
3. African Americans—Religion.   I. Hollies, Linda H.
BR563.N4S34 2007
253.082—dc22   2007030852

In Memoriam

~

Rev. Dr. Linda H. Hollies, sixty-four, noted author and United Methodist pastor, died unexpectedly on August 18, 2007, in Phoenix, Arizona. She was a prolific writer, popular speaker, and best-selling author of The Pilgrim Press, having written more than a dozen books for the Press. Dr. Hollies was in Phoenix on a book publicity tour to promote *Sister, Save Yourself! Direct Talk about Domestic Violence,* her most recent book before *Sage Sisters.* She was scheduled to preach at a local church the morning she died.

A favorite word of Dr. Hollies was "bodacious," a term she frequently used in her books to empower women. The word and the ideas associated with it became so popular with her fan base that *Publishers Weekly* had this to say: "Define bodacious as 'unmistakable, remarkable, and noteworthy' and you've a good working description of Hollies."

Dr. Hollies's numerous works are best summed up in her own words, written July 11, 2007: "As a woman of color, incest survivor, clergywoman, wife, mother, and grandmother, I have taken the 'stuff' of my own life, woven it together, by God's amazing grace, and I offer it to my sisters as a guide in every book. My work is intentionally self-revealing to detail how pain is fertilizer for growth into our best self."

She will be greatly missed by those who worked with her at The Pilgrim Press.

~

CONTENTS

❦ Contents ❧

⌒ DEDICATION

This book is dedicated to my personal counsel of life coaches:

Mama, Doretha Robinson Adams, Big Mama, Eunice Robinson Wade, Granny, Lucinda Robinson Weston, *my life sources;*

Barbara Jean Baker Vinson-Van Buren, *my "bestest-sista friend";*

Darlene Sims Lee and Elizabeth Clark Brown, *my school years' best friends;*

Ms. Ethel Sims, Ms. Catherine Jones, and Aunt Sweetie, *neighborhood "mothers";*

Thelma Nunn Pryor and Madine Blakley, *lifelong church sistas;*

Hortense House and Della Burt, *teachers/mentors and friends*

Emma Justes and Emilie Townes, *seminary professors and role models;*

JoClare Wilson and Cynthia Smitko, *CPE guides and pushers;*

Helen Marie Fannings Ammons and Marilyn Magee, *"sista-mothers" and friends;*

Linda Foster Mumson, Barbara Issacs, and Cecelia Long, *North Illinois path clearers;*

Ida Easley, Fran Brandon, and Brenda Heffner, *seminary prayer group;*

Marie Antoinette Carson, *great woman, good friend;*

Vera Jo Edington and Joyce E. Wallace, *Twinkling Butterfly Club;*

Harlene Harden, Beverly J. Garvin, Vanessa Stephens-Lee, Cynthia Belt, LaSandra Dolberry, Connie Wilkerson, Carolyn Wilkins, Juana Dunbar, and Carolyn Abrams, *who love me unconditionally;*

Valerie Bridgeman Davis and Geneieve Brown, *who were personal prophets in calling me to fly!*

Daisybelle Thomas Quinney, Janet Hopkins, *"Sisthurs";*

Eleanor L. Miller, *my pastor and intercessor;*

Mother Lucille Brown, Mother Ruby Earven, Mother Ray Margaret Jackson Hall, *my surrogate mothers, personal sages and bodacious women of wisdom!*

~ FOREWORD

It is our season and I am so glad that our Sista Linda has rounded up a collective of sages to share their stories. One of my favorite teaching books has always been *The Game of Life and How to Play It* by Florence Scovelle Chinn. It is one of the foundational books at Hillside Chapel, our worship and meditation center and at the Truth Center, where we hold our seminars and workshops. Within the pages of this book, we discover a variety of women who come forth in their own strength and energies to share how they came to know who they were and are in God. Each woman in her own unique way allows us to see that the first law of faith is to believe in what you say! Each woman is playing the game of life and playing it to win!

A few years ago, Sista Linda came to Hillside, calling women together from more than twenty denominations. The opening night of that holy convocation was held in our round sanctuary, where clergywomen, robed with such a variety of stoles, marching in harmony, brought a combined intellect and compassion that moved me to tears as I remembered my own nontraditional journey to ordained ministry. As I talked to my sisters and as I shared my pain, my joy, my journey, Sista Linda listened and declared that my story should be told. Today, I am working on that story and was delighted to be asked to write the forward for *Sage Sisters*.

People are hurting so badly, so desperately, and they simply want to be loved. We, women called by God, have the capacity and the will to love people to life. This is what *Sage Sisters* does; it offers unconditional love to sisters on the journey, detailing options, methods, alternative strategies to do ministry in a messed-up world. Women come to ministry bringing their minds, bodies, and souls. Women are involved and seeking to involve others in holistic living. Women don't stop creating beauty, networking, and offering pastoral care as they rise within the ranks. Our inclusive nature, our open hearts, and our generous spirits all shine forth as the women in this book become vulnerable at the request of Angela (whom you will be introduced to in the preface and who authors chapter 19), a sister to us all. How I wish that *Sage Sisters* had been available to me when I began this journey. How I wished that there had been women around for me to question about ordained ministry!

At age six, I had a vision of being in a pulpit. That call was affirmed for me when I was thirteen and a member, with my grandmother, at the historic Antioch Baptist Church in Houston, Texas. I remember going to talk to my pastor, Rev. T. J. Goodall, who promptly replied, "There is no place for women in ministry in a Baptist Church!" Yet I could teach Sunday school, sing in the choir, and do all the ministry open to women, and so I did. I went off to college at Texas Southern University to earn a degree in sociology but had to stop after my first year due to a bout with tuberculosis. I now realize that this was part of God's divine plan for my nontraditional path to ordination.

I was in the tuberculosis sanitarium for four years! Yes! I spent four years trying to get well. I was assigned to bed rest and medicines. From ages nineteen to twenty-three, I was in ministry with the black, female Baptist missionaries who came faithfully to offer Bible studies in our facility. Because my grandmother raised me, I knew the Bible. I was able to assist the missionaries until they began to depend upon me to step in for them at times. It was here that I "entered" ministry. I enjoyed serving people and was up, around, and everywhere in the sanitarium where there was a need. When I was released I went to complete my undergraduate degree and then went to Atlanta University for my master's degree, when Whitney Young was dean and Barbara Jordan and I were classmates. I worked as a maid to make up the difference from my rehabilitation grant. I begin to attend Wheat Street Baptist Church, under Rev. Wheat Borders, and was able to offer soft worship music, prayer, and meditation, as well as teaching the pastor's class. But it was never recognized as "ordained ministry." I was just working in the church.

After graduation, I went to Chicago and began work at the University of Chicago on my PhD. While struggling with my marriage and my son, Michael, I met a woman on the bus one day and began to share my story. She became my "Sage Brush." She invited me to her church, where Rev. Dr. Johnnie Coleman was pastor! I went, hungry and searching. I ended up attending, joining, and taking classes, and I eventually became director of Christian Education and Children's Ministries. Rev. King promoted me to be her administrator, and I learned much about the position of pastor. I told her that I had been called to ministry. She asked me, "What's stopping you?" She became another sage at that point and I was finally ordained into Unity.

One marriage ended, and another began as I married a Baptist pastor and moved with him and my son to Atlanta in 1971. I went to ITC to enroll in the Master's of Divinity program but was not accepted! I was a "first lady"! I went to work as the director of a mental health facility and began to teach Bible classes in our home on a weekly basis. Soon I had over fifty people coming to learn more about how to utilize the positive energies of God to center down, meditate, hear the Holy Spirit, and worship, in Spirit and in truth. Needless to say, my pastor spouse was not happy and that marriage ended, but I continued to draw professional people who were seeking into my teaching class.

The class kept growing and people began to drop offerings in a vase by my door. I went to work as dean of students at Spelman College and became known as "the swinging dean," for I took those students as my own and worked with them where they were. Eventually, I was forced out of my position due to my Wednesday night classes! It was said to be a "conflict of interest." I was not a pastor. I was a Bible teacher. But when they forced me out, I did call a group of the students of the Bible class. We organized, took their offerings, bought a small house, and became a nondenominational church! God used the "Living" section of the Atlanta newspaper to feature me and Hillside Chapel. This was just the boost that we needed. We bought a Presbyterian church and then decided to build our own church in the round. God has utilized all of my experiences and education in my call. For I do realize that being a pastor is being the executive director of a mental health facility!

Today, at age "seventy-fine," fine and fit, I am a sage! I can do everything that is done in any local congregation. I sing, play, usher, teach, preach, administrate, counsel, mentor, network, and refer. This is the game of life, and I do know how to play it! My answer to our sister, Angela, and my best sage advice to any woman in ministry is to pray, hear what God is saying, and then do it! Be that witness, use your intuitive wisdom, and be all that God has called you to become. Too many of us are led by the Holy Spirit but choose to go another way due to the ignorance of folks. The sages in this book have surely been there and done that! Not one of us needs a tee-shirt, for the reality of a call from God and the cost of the journey wears on our heart. I have come to know that the Holy Spirit is my source and I can wait on God in every situation to make a way out of no ways. This is the testimony within this book from sister to sister.

Sage Sisters covers it all for women in ordained ministry. Women share who have come through the traditional paths and those, like myself, who dared to do it in very nontraditional ways. The Sages tell us how to take it to the streets, for all souls belong to God and we are responsible for those in the house and those who are lost on the outside of our doors. The Sages share with us their understanding of ordination and go on to describe what the advent of a preaching woman looked like as she claimed God's voice for her own. There is so much diversity, so much variety within the voices of the Sages to help each one of us think clearer, rethink, remember and recall instances, people, and events that have made us who we have become. Read, reread and reread again the chapters that talk about beauty within God's house and on God's woman! I opened a boutique for tall women because all of us need to represent God, and God's house must be in order and it must be beautiful.

Sage Sisters offers us intimate insights into the call and the compelling reasons that many of us bring to the people of God. There is raw honesty, deep truth, compelling compassion, and the commitment to God that is required as we made our way in ministry. If you sense that you are called by God, if you are committed to the cause of the mission of Jesus Christ, then *Sage Sisters* will assist you in walking the talk as you represent God. We cannot talk good ministry. We must live excellent ministry. The stories within *Sage Sisters* provide details, strategies, and follow-through methods to be strong in God and in the power of God's might as we move forward.

Sage Sisters allows us to see that when we put prayer first and fear behind us, all things are possible. Planning, planning, and more planning is the key. A sage is always ready to make a move and open her doors with kindness and generosity, to whomever has a need.

When Minister Farrakhan came to Atlanta to install Minister Ava Muhammed as the first woman leader of a mosque, the school chosen for the service had an air conditioner failure. I opened the doors to Hillside and the installation service was held there. I and the women within Sage Wisdom are given to hospitality, even to the extreme. Today, at Hillside, we have more than three thousand in weekly worship, more than thirty working auxiliaries, and twenty-five classes during the week. A sage knows that she has to love people to life.

I know that you will enjoy reading *Sage Sisters*. I am assured that you will stretch, grow, and be challenged by the wisdom within its pages. I am impressed by the scholarship of our "teachers" who offer us their heart. And I'm in prayer for each one of them and for you as we continue this season of God using women in the world. For after thirty-five years, there are people who yet cannot and will not call me "Rev. King" or recognize my position as a pastor. We have many miles to go on this journey. When my mother, Mildred Shackleford, made her transition, she was a long-time member of the New Hope Baptist Church in Los Angles, California. She and her sisters were known as the singing Jackson Sisters. The pastor of the congregation is a classmate of mine. When Mama died, he called me to say, "Barbara, you know that we are Baptist. Although your mother loved and respected your ministry, you cannot speak from the pulpit here." The only way that I got to speak at my mothers' service was to give thanks to the people who came and participated!

The stories within *Sage Sisters* have encouraged my soul, have strengthened my spirit, and compel me to keep praying, hear what God is speaking to me, and go and do it! These sages have helped me to realize just how strong I have been down through the years, and just how many sisters I have had along the journey. I pray that this is only the first volume in a series, for there are more sages and many more stories that need to be told. I salute Sista Linda for this "first" edition.

—The Rev. Barbara Blake King

founder and pastor
Hillside Chapel and Truth Center
Atlanta, Georgia

∿ PREFACE

They take my kindness for weakness.
They take my silence for speechless.
They consider my uniqueness strange.
They call my language slang.
They see my confidence as conceit.
They see my mistakes as defeat.
They consider my success accidental.
They minimize my intelligence to "potential."
My questions mean "I'm unaware."
My advancement is somehow unfair.
Any praise is preferential treatment.
To voice concern is discontentment.
If I stand up for myself, I'm too defensive.
If I don't trust them, I'm too apprehensive.
I'm defiant if I separate.
I'm fake if I assimilate.
Yet, constantly I am faced with work place hate.
My character is constantly under attack.
Pride for my race makes me, "TOO BLACK."
Yet, I can only be me. And, who am I you might ask?
I am that Strong Black Person who stands on the backs of my
ancestor's achievements with an erect spine pointing to the stars
with pride, dignity, and respect, which lets the work place in
America know, that I not only possess the ability to play by the
rules, but I can make them as well!
Good, better, best. Never ever rest until YOUR good is better and
YOUR better is your best!

—Deborah A. Watts,
101 Ways to Know You're
"Black" in Corporate America

Her name is Angela. She was a seminarian at one of our local seminaries, Calvin Reformed. She's an African-American woman in a predominately Anglo setting. There were, however, about a dozen women enrolled and each one of them felt, out of place most of the time. For the Christian Reformed Church had only very recently been opened to ordain women for pastoral ministry. Angela has become an "angel" to my life. She's gifted as an artist. It was in this field that we met. She designed the worship bulletin for a service that I had been asked to lead at the Christian Reformed College for the Institute of Christian Worship.

Her name is Angela. She's a beautiful, mixed grey, braided-hair sister, who dresses in much African garb. She has multiple sclerosis (MS) and often uses a mobile unit for travel. Yet, this has not stopped her from answering God's call to ordained ministry and enrolling in seminary, although many of her family members and friends think that she's simply "going through the change of life"! This call to ministry, however, is not new to Angela. What's new is becoming "official" with her ministry.

Her name is Angela. For many years in her community, she and her husband had been leaders in a coffeehouse ministry that met in an apartment complex. The space was free; she and Raymond set up each week, bought the snacks, and then cleaned up. She sings a cappella. She writes and recites poems. She draws, designs, makes cards, stationary, and of course, worship bulletins. She is an awesome representative of God's creativity. She's a gatherer of people. She's an exceptional student. She's wise, innovative, and ready to step out and lead a congregation. So she asked me, on behalf of her peers, "Linda, what do we do after graduation?"

Her name is Angela. In the middle of the world, "sanctified" there she stands, eyes wide open, facing forward, enthused and willing to move to the next level. However, there are a precious few role models for her to seek out. There are not many women in her denomination who can declare, "Been there! Done that!" So it's time for a book on some of the essential things that every woman in ministry needs to know!

Her name is Angela. She is the very first African American woman to graduate from Calvin Theological Seminary, in the city of Grand

Rapids, Michigan! She graduated in May of 2005 and has been ordained to a pastoral position at Church of the Servant in the Christian Reformed denomination. She is seeking to do ministry around the issues of racial reconciliation, inclusion, and intentional development of interracial relationships within congregations. There are no books, no courses, and no quick and easy available resources for our sister to access today. Therefore, *Sage Sisters* has been compiled, especially for Angela and for the other sisters who need to know what to anticipate in ordained ministry.

The intent of *Sage Sisters* is for use in seminaries as a teaching tool and to offer female students viable options in and out of the parish settings. *Sage Sisters* is also to help our male counterparts more fully appreciate what we go through when we dare to respond to God's call on our lives. And *Sage Sisters* is to be a record, chronicling some of the craziness that we have all experienced while feeling, "I'm the only one this has happened to in life!"

I've called for the sages! I've gathered the sage, wise women pastors, professors, heads of religious organizations, and other female leaders who have been the strong warriors braving the challenges, making the strides, leading the way so that other women pastors won't have it as difficult when they come on the scene. Many of us have served as associates, ministers of music, director of education, professors of religion, and other nonpastoral positions. We are the very ones who have done the "grunt work" and have been "the clean-up women" in too many congregations. Therefore, in *Sage Sisters* we will count choirs, youth groups, women's studies, and classes as congregations!

We are all aware that what we learned in seminary did not prepare us for life with a congregation, whether in a local parish, classroom, or educational venue. *Sage Sisters* will not be the definitive word from women clergy to women clergy. For we continue to enter this sacred journey at differing paths. So, those whose stories are contained within *Sage Sisters* will act as signposts for our journey. None of us know exactly where we will end up, but we can stand, read, identify, and say, "Well, here I stand!" *Sage Sisters* is an offering of living water in the midst of the desert journey that offers all of us an oasis for reflection and refreshment. *Sage Sisters* will help each of us to better cope as those always present "clergy killers" make serious attempts to turn us into tumbling tumbleweeds!

What *Sage Sisters* will do is to remind all of us that there are no perfect congregations, no perfect locations, no perfect officers, and no perfect pastors! We are followers on the journey that was laid out years ago by Moses and Jocobed, Abraham and Sarah, Joseph and Rachel as well as Jesus and his disciples. "They" tried and often did kill these people of God. But then, God has never promised us an easy journey, although we have wished it to be so!

~ ACKNOWLEDGMENTS

That you may know . . . what are the riches of God's glorious inheritance among the saints, and what is the immeasurable greatness of God's power for us who believe . . . (Eph. 1:18–19). These few pages are to acknowledge more of the vast and wonderful network of folk who have touched my life, shared their love, care, prayers, and wise counsel with me. Several pages could not contain their names. An entire book could not hold their gifts to my life. And only eternity will be able to reveal my "riches of God's glorious inheritance" of kin, friend, and family. I owe each one named untold gratitude.

A book is never written in isolation. All the persons who touch, influence, inspire, and even hinder your life help you in the writing process. The lessons you have learned and the individuals who taught you hover over your shoulders, waiting to see if you mastered the materials. In the same way that "it takes a village to raise a child," it takes your entire life community to write a book.

I'm thankful to my "life community" for my personal experiences and awareness of my journey. Many are the charitable and gracious souls who have loved me, caught me, and forgiven me when I have stumbled, blundered, and just plain messed up! I have been picked up, lifted up, forgiven, and blessed to grow and to become by my "life community."

My family of origin heads this list of folks who helped to write every one of my books. My grandmothers, Lucinda Weston, Eunice Wade, Ethel Kellom, and Lessie Bell King, live in me, speak to me, and continue to admonish and cheer me as they watch from the realms of glory. My Big Daddy, Dock Wade, is with them and I appreciate the loving role modeling he provided. My parents, James and Doretha Adams, gave me life and granted me the necessary lessons that have taught me to hold on to God's unchanging hand! My aunt, Barbara Weston, taught me by example the art of meditation, relaxing, releasing, and letting go of yesterday's pain. My uncle, her spouse, Clenton Weston, taught me how to be there for family.

Finally, there is my father in ministry, Rev. James A. Anderson, who opened the doors to professional ministry to me, and his wife, Hardina, who applauded my ministry efforts and pushed my books. My girlfriends who have joined the heavenly cheerleaders include Darlene Sims Lee, Rev. Dr. Janet Hopkins, Pastor Connie Wilkerson, and Evangelist Thelma Nunn Pryor. Also, one of my young cheerleader brothers, Rev. Dr. Dennis Robinson, was called into eternity recently. All of these now await me on the "other side." I simply pray that I teach their lessons of wisdom well. Truly, they all invested in and taught me with their lives.

My siblings and extended family are the rich soil that has nurtured my soul. For Jacqui, Bob, Troy Sr., Kristy, and Troy Jr.; Riene, Tony, Lynne, Ciera and Ashante; Michael and Missy; Regina, Arthur, Raymond, Darling, Journey Ibn, and Millicent; James Jr., Jeanette, Noah, and Mohanna; Eddie, Onnette, Eddie Jr., and Candance; David, Kim, Dave Jr., and Ean; and Robert Tyrone and Lisa, I give God thanks and praise.

My husband, Mista Chuck, is my soul mate and best friend; my daughter, Grian Eunyke, her sons, Giraurd and Gamel, her daughter, Symphony; my oldest son, Gregory Raymond Everett, and my "baby boy," Grelon Renard Everett, who is now flute playing in eternity, have each taught me lessons and learned life because of me. As family we know better how to love and to forgive, unconditionally.

My "family" is another name for Love! Mista Chuck's children have included me and mine in their family circle over these thirty-plus years and Wisdom demands that I name them: Pam and Erin, JoAnne, Paul, Lacie, Michael, Imani, Cory, and Darian "Bear"; Donna Marie, Ronald Charles, Anita, and Jordan.

There are children of my womb and there are daughters of my heart: Angie Hooks, Jacqui Ford, Tracy Flaggs, Darlene Webster, and Sandy Adams. There are brothers who have helped me along life's winding road and made my life easier. These are Da Boys, my colleagues, brothers and friends, who always have my back: Dr. Zawdie K. Abiade (and Nancy), Apostle Anthony Earl (and Rev. Bobbie), Dr. Michael Carson (and Rev. Katherine), Dr. Dennis Robinson (and Rev. Darlene), and Dr. Donald Guest (and Brenda).

❧ Acknowledgments ❧

I have some primary cheerleaders who pump me up and call me to write "on demand." I so appreciate Kim Martin Sadler, my editor and friend, and the loving staff at The Pilgrim Press; Linda Peavy of Judson Press, who has pulled me to many places; Kris Firth, my copy editor, who makes better use of my long sentences and exclamation marks! Rev. Marge, Phil, and Azariah Bermann, along with Rev. Cynthia Stewart, Rev. Dr. Michelle Lloyd-Paige, Rev. Linda Male, and Pastor Carolyn Wilkins keep me grounded. My sisters at the Gathering Table, an e-mail encounter-support group, founded by Rev. La Sandra Dolberry, of San Diego, California, are my steadfast prayer group. I bless each and every one of them for hanging tough!

Truly, I give thanks to God for an awesome beautician who not only hooks up my hair and keeps the grey away, but also ministers to me with her laying on of hands as well as with dazzling homemade quilted wall hangings, Mrs. Pamela Tardy of Turning Heads Boutique.

These, plus my congregation at Calvary UMC in Jackson, Michigan, are the folks who are responsible for me being the bodacious, wise woman that I am today. I have been touched, impacted, and inspired by their lives. For each of them and many more, I give God total praise! My prayer is that they, too, are always surrounded by Wisdom's counsel so that they will reap the sage wisdom that carries us to multiple harvests of blessings!

Finally, I give God thanks for YOU, my readers, who keep buying my books, raising questions, sending e-mail, cards, and letters that stimulate another book. It's amazing to me that the Holy Spirit continues to endow me with the wisdom and knowledge that allows me to "write the vision and to make it plain upon pages" that others might read. I count myself privileged, blessed, and highly favored to have this precious opportunity and I don't take it lightly. Thank you for walking this journey with me.

—*Shalom! Sista Linda*

WHEN MAMA WAS GOD

When mama was God
She made miracles happen
    In the middle of a Houston ghetto
    The center of my universe, indeed, when mama was God
She walked on water
    in three-inch heels, matching bag
    With us five kids in her footsteps.
    When mama was God
She taught us to fear not
    night lighting, thunderstorms
    hard work, new things, good success.
When mama was God
She treated not one but two
    fancy Easter dresses and sewed lace on my socks to match.
She hollered for me from the porch
    compelling me to come out, come out
    from all my favorite hiding places.
She held me so close with strong hands
    so close that I would inhale
    warm fleshy bosom heat for air.
When mama was God
She stood her ground with white folk
    those blue-eyed devils of pure evil
    of the 60s . . . 80s . . . this new millennium.
She laid hands on us/me
    so the cops wouldn't and trifling men couldn't
    halting bad attitudes and healing broken hearts.
She made a dollar holla
    on the occasion of more month than money
    without robbing anyone of anything.
When mama was God
She blessed two fish and five loaves
    or was that govm't cheese and canned mystery meat?
She always kept an open door policy
    always meant that somebody else
    would be sleeping on the living room floor.

She prayed for us and many others
    we eavesdropped listening for our name
    knowing that no weapon formed against
    us would prosper.
When mama was God.
SELAH*
"Girl, you just like your mama,"
    somebody said that day
    when I was feeling a whole lot like God!

—Raedorah Stewart-Dodd

*SELAH: *pause and think about it/amen. A biblical musical notation of interlude, pause, pondering in the Psalms.*

Sage Wisdom *about*

Ordained Ministry

I ❧ WRESTLING WITH ORDINATION

M. Francis Manning

Baptist Church

I feel myself turning the corner. After nine months of chaotic silence, the desire to hear my thoughts out returned today. I woke up with an appetite for a well thought-out thought. I started a book this morning, with the words, "For everything I have learned there has been a season for getting it done." The season of my melancholy appears to be rapidly vanishing. The storm is passing over. Hallelujah!!

A miracle isn't a miracle because it defies explanation. A miracle is a miracle because it is experienced as a miracle. It happened at the time when I needed grace most, namely, on the last day for miracles.

—Renita Weems, *Listening for God:*
A Minister's Journey through Silence and Doubt

Much conversation has been had about what is crucial to ordained ministry. This is good conversation because ordination is not the routine, habitual, perfunctory, everyday entrée to a professional career in ministry, or the reward for faithful service that it is often perceived to be. To be turned into a church factotum, where we attempt to be everything to everybody, through this ancient process was probably the farthest thought from God's mind.

Like others, I have many thoughts about the very act of ordination along with the other accompanying processes that are required. Many of my personal thoughts are yet unvoiced. There are many of them that have arisen through the years. This book is a good place to wrestle with my own thoughts.

It is felt that Jesus ordained his disciples and that the apostles picked up the practice. Because ordination has various scriptural warrant, some believe it confers on recipients a special character that remains with them for life. Some think that ordination protects the church. Still others think that ordination transmits particular grace for the pastoral office; that it conveys particular license not granted to others. Others define ordination as an impressive sign of the apostolic succession that confers spiritual authority, limiting the theology of the priesthood of all believers.

Among us Baptists, ordination is the setting apart of a person divinely called to a work of special service in the church. Thus, we are empowered to bless babies, baptize believers, marry the living, bury the dead, administer the ordinances, equip the saints, and manage the local church.

What we have done as a denomination is to formulate a theology of ordination that is compatible with a Protestant doctrine of the ministry. Ordination is accepted almost universally as a legitimate rite of the church; but attempts to define its significance or necessity do not reveal the uncertain foundations upon which it is based.

Although scripture is called upon to substantiate many of these assumptions, contradictory opinions about ordination continue to exist. One of the reasons for this is that the King James Version of scripture uses "ordain" to translate over twenty Hebrew and Greek words that relate a variety of ideas such as God's work and providence; the appointment to an office or task; and the establishment of laws, principles, places, or observances. All these ideas do not relate directly to ordination but they do contain basic concepts of divine purpose, divine choice, divine appointment, and a divine institution that undergirds the practice. We can't hope to even begin to understand them all. But in an attempt to get a fresh handle on this, trusting that I don't "stir up more snakes than I can kill," I ask that you walk with me for a spell. Remember, I'm wrestling with this concept.

There are four primary Old Testament examples that provide precedent for ordination: (1) the consecration of Aaron and his sons as priests; (2) the dedication of the Levites as servants of God; (3) the appointment of seventy elders to assist Moses, and, finally, (4) the commission of Joshua as Moses' successor. The ordination of the priest was based on God's choice of Aaron and his sons according to Exodus 28:1 that they would minister to God in the priest's office. The ordination itself was a seven-day act of consecration accompanied by washing, putting on certain vestments, anointing, sacrificing, and eating. The basic Hebrew term for ordination in this context literally meant filling the hands and may have referred to filling the priest's hand with offerings. At the least it meant filling the hand from God's hand to do the work that God had assigned him to do. If we accept this as normative, then it's quite permissible to say that ordination is the filling of one's hands to do a work for God; it is the sanctifying of one's hands as instruments of service. This is a far cry from some of our contemporary understandings of ordination.

The ordination of the Levites was also accompanied by the laying on of hands of the whole congregation, offering the Levites as a wave offering and sacrifices unto God. If we accept this as normative then at the least it is expected that there will be a clear affirmation from a local congregation that an individual is indeed being ordained by God and then presented as a wave offering who is willingly offering service back to God.

The appointment of the seventy to assist Moses in bearing the burden of the people as recorded in Numbers 11:17 was at God's initiative through his father-in-law, Jethro. Moses selected persons to be known as elders and leaders. Their ordination involved standing with Moses and receiving from God the Spirit that was previously upon Moses. When the Spirit rested on them they were able to begin to prophesy. The ordination of a successor for Moses was at Moses' initiative, but Joshua was chosen by God and filled with the Spirit.

Joshua's ordination involved standing before the priest and all of the congregation and being commissioned in their sight. Moses laid his hand on Joshua, and Moses placed some of his authority on Joshua, including the role of inquiry of the judgment of the Urim and Thummin. If this is the norm, then a leader has the right to choose and ordain his or her successor in ministry. Some of my Baptist colleagues would dispute this right given our congregational polity of democratic rule.

When Jesus appointed the twelve that he might send them forth to preach, this was based on prayer, his choice, and call. Nowhere in scripture do we find a formal ordination service. The same is true of the seventy whom Jesus sent out to minister. The Great Commission was given solely on the basis of Jesus' power and authority. He did not ask "the congregation" what they thought. The Holy Spirit was given to them directly without laying on of hands. But then that was Jesus.

Several other New Testament passages describe appointments without reference to ordination. Having been chosen by lot, Matthias was installed as one of the twelve. Barnabas and Paul appointed elders in every church after prayer and fasting. Titus was left in Crete to perform the same function.

Several other passages describe ordination as being accompanied by the laying on of hands by Paul and the assembly of elders. In Jerusalem Barnabas and Paul, who were already prophets and teachers, were set apart for a missionary work to which God had called them. Timothy was chosen by prophecy, recommended by Paul, and ordained to his task by the laying on of hands by Paul and the assembly of elders.

The reference to the prophets and teachers ministering unto God and fasting is not to be passed over lightly in Acts 13:1–3. The word for worship, *leitourgein*, is used in the Septuagint of the cultic priest and the Levite. The usual word here would be *diakonia* (service) but Luke avoids it. The implication of these allusions to the Levites for the mission of Paul and Barnabas is indeed helpful. The laying on of hands on these two was neither to recognize gifts for leadership nor to commission them for service; such was not necessary. They were setting out to mediate the New Covenant to the peoples, both Jew and Gentile. They were being given the priestly authority to do so.

The possibility even exists that the body of believers as a whole laid hands on Barnabas and Paul. Allusions to the laying on of hands of the Levites in Numbers 8:15 lend force to this argument. The importance of context is laid before us here. Luke's Old Testament connection is not always apparent in English translations, but it is still important. These events are temporally conditioned, which gives them their significance.

The lack of a consistent biblical pattern raises so many questions in some circles about ordination today. Who should be ordained? Why? By whom? On the basis of what qualifications? What do they receive in the act of ordination? We will never be able to answer all these questions, for they will vary with the biblical model assumed and continue to be debated in various denominations.

On the other hand, because there is no consistent biblical pattern, we need not see this as a hindrance rather as an occasion to shop in what I call God's ecclesiastical boutique and find there all that is needed to equip us for service.

We can thrash around about ordination, how we do it, to whom do we do it, and why we do it, but the ultimate essential is this—

unless the Holy Spirit sets the seal of service upon someone, it is to no avail. For you see, when we are "sho nuf" separated to serve, some things are going to come into one's life that human wisdom cannot handle, that human power cannot manage, that no human power can discern. When we are separated to serve we may lay hands and acknowledge the call, but God is the one who has already done the separating. Consequently the work of calling and ordaining belong to God.

I believe that there are a few more essentials. When you're separated to serve you can't ever take yourself so seriously that you think the work belongs to you. The sooner we begin to acknowledge that this is God's work and God's work alone, the sooner we'll begin to experience major victories in our ministry life. The longer it takes us to realize that, the less victory we'll see. When you're separated to serve there will often be periods of loneliness, even with people all around you. When you're separated some of your old friends are not going to know what to do with you anymore. If you're truly walking with Jesus Christ, some will walk away from you . . . even some of the saved ones. Beware of why your new friends want to be your new friends. Their agenda might not be yours. Love people but trust God. Remember the words that we believe were those of Christ hidden in the Old Testament: "Where did I get these wounds? In the house of my friend" (Zech. 13:6); "My own familiar friend has lifted up his heel against me" (Psa. 41:9).

This may sound like paranoia, but you've got to watch your back, watch your front, watch your sides, and always, by all means, "CYA." Keep on the whole armor. But don't get too hung up on this; maintain balance. The same God who separated you and called you will sustain you. You won't always know what to do or what to say beforehand but trust this: God will always provide what you need when you need it and not before. Walk with God and God will walk with you.

Here is another essential nugget for my seminary trained "sistas." Men are jealous but so are women. Those who are less educated will make cracks and throw off on you about your education. They never consider the fact that you have been blessed by God to be seminary educated, not to lord it over them, but so you can love God with your mind and serve the church with knowledge and information. Stop apologizing for your blessings. Paradigms are shifting and changing. The church needs those who are equipped in other than traditional ways to accommodate those shifts.

You're going to have to learn to deal with the faces. What do I mean by that? There are people who are good at putting on faces for you to see and for other people to see. If they approve of what you're saying they'll smile at you. If they don't they'll scowl at you They will make sure that some impressionable others see it either way. But as God told Jeremiah when he was called, "Do not be afraid of their faces" (Jer. 1:8).

Why are people still like this in days of enlightenment when mostly everybody can read the Bible and discover for themselves whether God has called women or not? Because even though "they" say the Bible is authoritative, "they" won't let the Bible speak authoritatively. When permitted to speak for itself and not be subjected to what I call the "Supermarket Syndrome," where interpreters and expositors get to throw into their hermeneutical carts what best suits their finicky, selective appetites, the Bible authenticates women in ministry, especially in the Old Testament.

It's not good enough for your ministry to rest on tired, worn-out clichés like "if God can use a donkey he can use a woman" or "the men won't go so God is sending women." In principle these may be true; but God's purpose in using women is said better and finds its origin in the pages of the Old Testament, in that foundational book Genesis.

The opening pages provide us with our first clue, where chapter 1, verse 26, tells us that Adam was made in the image of God. Verse 27's "God created him" is parallel to the following clause "God created them," indicating that the "him" is synonymous with the "them." The "Adam" is both a male and a female. Thus Adam could be translated human or humanity. It is called synecdoche, or one standing for all. Adam is a singular that represents the plural male and female. If Adam is made in the image of God, then male and female have been made in the image of God. Conversely, in order to understand God's nature, males and females together are needed to reflect God's image. The image of God is a double image. There is no possibility, then, according to these verses, that Adam the male could by himself reflect the nature of God. So then, foundationally, ordination is essentially God filling the hands of God's creation with authority to serve the body of Jesus Christ and the world. Today, we merely acquiesce to God's original plan. How humbling is this?

Well, I didn't give a concrete answer to Sista Angela, but I'm privileged to have had the opportunity to wrestle with my own ordination and hopefully provide each of us the benefit of my own seminary and pastoral training. I know that God called me. I know that God uses me. My ordination was just confirmation. I pray that yours is the same.

2 ∾ I Didn't Sign Up for This!

Gina Casey

African Methodist Episcopal Zion

Racism also figures in why Black women are often quiet about the inequities found within the Christian church. Even though it is clearly women who form the church's backbone—filling the pews, organizing the fundraisers, cooking the dinners, and teaching Sunday School—in a large number of churches across the country, women are barred from standing in the pulpit and attaining other positions of leadership. Still, they do not often complain, hesitant to disrupt the one place that has traditionally been a safe harbor for Black women, their refuge from racial cruelty, and the one institution where Black men have been consistently empowered and affirmed . . . thus, in their daily lives, the overwhelming reality of racism pressures many Black women, often unconsciously, to suppress their concerns about gender discrimination.

—Charisse Jones, Kumea Shorter-Gooden,
Shifting: The Double Lives of Black Women in America

None of my responses were satisfactory. The bishop was interrogating me and challenging everything I was saying in my defense. My presiding elder caught a mysterious case of amnesia when the bishop asked him if it was true that I had sought his counsel and followed his recommendation to join another church in the district after being dismissed from the ministerial staff of my former church.

"Uh, I don't remember, Bishop."

"How on earth can you stand there and say that?" For that retort, the Bishop declared me rude and disrespectful in front of what seemed like hundreds in attendance at the annual conference.

The bishop had previously stated that anyone pursuing an MBA instead of an M.Div. was not serious about his or her calling. *Was he for real?* The pastor who was trying to strip me of my ordination at

9

this conference was the same one who, five months prior, fired me from my job at the church and relieved me of my ministerial duties. I was married and had three children. Finding secular employment was the quickest and most logical way to contribute to the household budget.

Like actors who serve tables while auditioning and awaiting their big break, most ministers have to hold down secular jobs, especially in the early years of their ministry. In fact, 80 percent of the pastors and 99 percent of the associate ministers in that conference were holding secular jobs. Our denomination was not in the practice of providing funds for its ministers to attend seminary. My new corporate job, however, was paying three times more than the church and offering 100 percent tuition reimbursement. (Last time I looked, a Master of Divinity was still not on their list of majors acceptable for reimbursement.) So how could the bishop publicly reprimand me for taking advantage of a free education opportunity?

The next response was an Episcopal tirade against me and all other preachers who lack seriousness and go into ministry for all the wrong reasons. This was terrible. I was standing, facing the bishop, and being made a spectacle of before my peers and the laity. I honestly could not have been more embarrassed if I were standing there naked before the masses. The harangue seemed unending. Would it end favorably? Surely God will not allow this guy to destroy my ministry? He had already successfully convinced my husband that I was out of control and he was, therefore, justified in firing me. Surely God would not let this man succeed in breaking up my home. Is this what ministry was all about? Is this what I signed up for?

Don't get me wrong. I did not walk into ministry with my eyes shut. I had been in church all my life. I knew there would be challenges from men and women who felt that "female preachers" were biblically and socially oxymoronic. Growing up Baptist, I initially thought that my biggest hurdle would be the reaction of my family to the news of my calling. The matriarchs (namely, my mom, grandmothers, and mother-in-law) were extremely supportive. My precious father, a Baptist minister, changed his theology after I shared the news. "Who am I to disagree with God?" he replied with a smile and a hug. Even my husband told me that he was okay with me being called to preach. The only negative reaction came from my aunt: "Just one more preacher taking the poor people's money!" I was acquainted with her experience with at least one dishonest pastor. But I did not have a reputation for being deceitful, so her remark really stung. Nevertheless, the majority of my family was behind me, and that was enough.

A commitment to doing the will of God in becoming a minister would not only be challenging from the perspective of gender, but I realized it might also cause a flurry of satanic activity against me. I contemplated these and other consequences while grappling with the decision to say "yes" to God. I thought I had anticipated all of the worst scenarios possible.

I had not considered this, however.

Before this man was my pastor, we were members of the same church. My eldest child is his godson. I was twenty-three and he was thirty-nine when he was called to preach. Shortly thereafter, he felt led to start a new church within our denomination and asked my husband and me to join him. Since we were friends, my husband and I agreed. We worked diligently in the new ministry, taking on any and every position necessary to ensure its success. Even though we were not in complete agreement with every pastoral decision and action, we still submitted to the authority of our spiritual leader. So when this "friend" intentionally sought to destroy my ministry and credibility, I was stunned. His actions resulted in peers, friends, and family members turning their backs on me. Words cannot adequately describe the magnitude of the pain I felt as I told God, tearfully, "I didn't sign up for this!"

It took a while for me to realize something interesting about accepting assignments from God. The sheer genius of the divine call is in God's ability to secure human commitment after revealing only a glimpse of the assignment, the very tip of the iceberg. I wonder if Moses would have said "yes" to God if he had known that, one day, his beloved siblings would turn against him. What if he had foreknown the depths of stubbornness, obstinacy, faithlessness, grumblings, and rebelliousness in the hearts of the children of Israel?

How would Moses have responded knowing the countless times he would have to intercede before God on their ungrateful, trifling behalf? What if he foreknew, after forty years of bailing out the Israelites over and over again, that they would eventually provoke him to such an extent that he would find himself numbered among those prohibited from entering into the promised land? Is this really what he signed up for? If the apostles understood that they would have to endure horrific persecution for the sake of this man who called them to forsake all and follow him, would they have so readily accepted Jesus' invitation? If they had been privy to just 10 percent of what awaited them on the other side of "Yes, God!" would the Gospels and Acts contain the same apostolic accounts? Did they really sign up to undergo the terrible sufferings they experienced? Would the revelation of their future tribulations have changed their initial responses in any way?

I can only answer for myself. In my case, the future had to remain hidden. God, in God's infinite wisdom, knew that I would *never* have accepted the calling to preach if I had been aware of the things I would have to endure for the sake of preaching the gospel. Yet, in what other way could God have prepared me for decades of ministry? Yes, I went through a devastating experience during the early years of my ministry. However, with God's help, I survived! In hindsight, I can see that it served to make me wiser, and to strengthen and equip me for future ministerial assignments and circumstances. Among other things, I was being prepared for the challenges of being a senior pastor. God was grooming me to successfully cope with the pain and heartbreak of hurting people, dying members, being betrayed by my leaders, their loss of faith in me, my loss of faith in myself. Whether struggling through the implementation of a difficult or unpopular decision at my church, or standing my ground before bishops and denominational leaders, remembering how God has prepared me for these situations gives me the strength and boldness necessary for enduring success.

To date, nothing in ministry has come close to the painful, humiliating confrontation I faced eighteen years ago. No, I did not sign up for it. Yet, I did agree to give my all to Jesus, come what may. I did agree to lay down my life for God. I did agree to put my hand to the plow and never turn back. Through a mighty move of God, the evil intent of a prideful pastor was thwarted in divine resplendence during that annual conference. My ordination was never lifted. Writing about this nearly two decades later, it is quite evident that what was designed to destroy me actually served to make me wiser in Christ Jesus and empowered me for future ministry.

A job offer from Intel opened the door for me to leave Maryland in 1993. My family and I pulled up stakes and moved to Phoenix,

Arizona. At the time of my departure, I had received my second of two ordinations in the African Methodist Episcopal Zion Church and was associating at Trinity AME Zion in Washington, D.C. As an ordained elder, I promised my bishop that I would introduce myself to an AME Zion church in Phoenix upon my arrival. But deep within the recesses of my heart, I was still a wounded soldier, and a brief hiatus from God's service seemed more than reasonable.

I had decided that I would keep my promise to the bishop, but become AWOL after the initial church visit. Soon I would learn that there was only one AME Zion church in the entire state of Arizona: Fisher Chapel. It is located in the South Mountain community and, at that time, direct faced an open field of desert weeds, diseased cacti, and vermin. The houses of the neighborhood were old but generally well kept. I found out that people living in wealthier neighborhoods were afraid to venture to South Mountain neighborhoods because of the reputation for drug activity and violence. I drove up to Fisher Chapel for the first time on the fourth Sunday in May 1993. Surveying the area, I thought, "What, in heaven's name, would possess a person to plant a church here?" I parked and entered the sanctuary (which is now our fellowship hall). The temperature outdoors was in the low 100s and there was no air conditioning inside. As I took a seat in one of the many available metal folding chairs, I also took in the scene: small sanctuary, homemade pulpit, a very skinny preacher singing out of tune, a female associate minister (his wife?), no musician, no choir, less than twenty adults and children in attendance, barefoot toddlers donning only diapers, and stifling heat.

Nope, I'm not coming back here! Next Sunday, I'll disappear among the worshippers at that big Baptist church downtown!

The sermon ended and the preacher extended the invitation for Christian discipleship. On automatic, I went and sat on the empty piano bench and began playing a hymn. (Needless to say, it is really unwise to call attention to one's talents when intent on not returning.) Before the benediction, the visitors were asked to stand and I introduced myself, minus clerical title. That is when God blew my cover. A woman on the left side of the church—who turned out to be the wife of the senior pastor, who was absent that day—stood up and said, "We've been expecting you! The bishop said you were coming and you'd help us out!"

All I really wanted, God, was a brief reprieve. Was that too much to ask? What on earth did I do to deserve this? I have already experienced involvement in a small church. Why, God, why? You know that I did not sign up for this!

I cried all the way back to my apartment. Clearly, I could neither run nor hide from God. So I found a place of frustrated obedience as the church pianist and associate minister.

In 1994, we moved into a small but beautiful sanctuary built adjacent to the former place of worship. A year later, the presiding bishop of the Western Episcopal District decided to move our founding pastor from Phoenix to Los Angeles. Since I was the only other AME Zion minister within a four-hundred-mile radius, I was the pastoral heir apparent. I was in Beaverton, Oregon, on assignment at Intel, when I received a call from my husband. He told me that the bishop wanted me to contact him and that I was going to be asked to consider a pastoral appointment to Fisher Chapel. I struggled to find a correct response before contacting the bishop. You must realize that I *never* desired to pastor a church. I wanted to be an evangelist and travel to different places, preaching the word and then leaving without the burden of developing and maintaining lasting relationships with the hearers. The notion of falling in love with a congregation and then seeing some of them leave the church because they had become angry and frustrated was wholly unappealing. Or, even worse, watching members grow ill and die. No, I *definitely* didn't sign up for this! If I had to preach the gospel in order to be obedient to God's calling upon my life, then I had intended to take the "easy" road, avoiding the pastorate altogether. Even though I accepted the appointment, the nagging question in the back of my mind was, "Did I *really* just sign up for this?"

Prior to relocating to a church in California, the founding pastor had told me I would not be able to maintain Fisher Chapel's relationships with most of the Phoenix churches because their pastors were not receptive to women ministers. I told him it would be their loss. To this day, I can only identify one church that has ended its relationship with us since I became pastor.

In Methodism, there is only one pastoral appointment per church, and it is not an autonomous position. The leadership to whom pastors are accountable (that is, bishops and presiding elders) is predominately male and not without its gender biases. Clergywomen, therefore, tend to have a greater challenge overall because the playing field never seems to be quite level with that of our male peers. As a matter of fact, I have faced gender challenges, literally, from the time I accepted God's call to ministry. This "good old boy" culture is reminiscent of my experience in the corporate world. At one point, I was the only African American manager in my department at Intel. I experienced extreme frustration dealing with racial and gender issues while in that position. Here were two different arenas—one secular, one religious—but the same fight. In both arenas, win or lose, I gained a reputation of refusing to back down from a fight against an injustice. Interestingly, I found myself regularly being asked to mentor both businesswomen and clergywomen who were also struggling with these issues. In hindsight, I see this as a time when the Holy Spirit began expanding my ministry to include women inside and outside the church.

While championing the cause of gender equality, God was subtly making attitudinal adjustments within me. To be honest, I had my own prejudices to overcome. I hated dealing with anyone who was petty or catty or insecure, and it seemed the feminine gender was saturated with more than its fair share of people dominated by these attributes. As a result, I rarely participated in women's groups or gatherings. One exception, however, was an annual women's retreat that was put on by my former church in Washington, D.C. I endured the fashion shows and beauty sessions (which they always seemed to include), but I thoroughly enjoyed the biblical teachings and the seminars on entrepreneurship and financial independence. The presenters were eloquent, strong, and confident, yet very feminine. An opportunity to chat with any one of them was a major bonus—one after which I intentionally sought each year. Every retreat left me feeling more empowered and self-assured. So, as a new pastor, when I realized the need for my female parishioners to experience an increase in confidence and self-esteem, I was strongly impressed that a women's retreat was the answer.

During the planning of our first retreat in Phoenix, I found myself driven by an overwhelming desire to make a marked difference in the lives of the women of Fisher Chapel, as well as in the lives of their female family members and friends. I appointed a retreat committee, but none of them had ever attended one. With the help of the Holy Spirit, I created what would become the blueprint for an annual event designed to encourage and empower women through spiritual teachings, interactive workshops, and lots of laughter. Our first year presenters were my personal friends, women of God who had exhibited strength in leadership and a true love for sisterhood. God gave me an idea about how to ensure this event would not be just another information dump onto paying, note-taking participants.

Every attendee, including presenters, received a preretreat package, which included the name of a specific woman of the Bible. Their task was to research and prepare a three- to five-minute creative presentation on this biblical character for the other attendees. Initially, the participatory assignment met with some resistance, especially from those who were especially shy or felt they were not biblically astute enough to present anything to a bunch of churchwomen. But, in the end, each woman benefited from doing her research and everyone did an exceptional job. Over the years, God has used these "participatory assignments"—which are completely different each year, usually complementing the retreat theme—to draw us closer in Christian sisterhood by providing glimpses into the personal life and character of each attendee. We return after each retreat appreciating one another, thoroughly convinced that there is more that unites than divides us. For the past ten years, at the conclusion of each retreat, my love for sisterhood grows deeper and stronger.

Today, I treasure my position as pastor of a vibrant and loving congregation. I count it an honor and a privilege to be chosen by God and trusted to provide spiritual leadership to such wonderful women and men who desire to do great things in the name of Christ Jesus.

After eleven years, I am still the only AME Zion pastor in Arizona. I sit on several conference boards and denominational committees, to which I would never have been appointed had I not left the great number of AME Zion ministers of the Philadelphia-Baltimore Conference. In 2004, my bishop appointed me academic dean of the Leadership Training Institute of the Western Episcopal Area. Because of God's favor, my clerical peers, both male and female, as well as our Episcopal leaders, respect me. Today, male and female clerical peers, including those who had previously deemed me unworthy of God's call to ministry, respect me. When I left Maryland, I thought I was running away from a hurtful past.

But what I was actually running toward was a future filled with opportunities to help others heal from the hurts of their pasts. I know, personally, what it means to be betrayed, to be filled with deep despair, to feel abandoned by God and humanity. As a result of these experiences, now I am able to listen with empathy to those who need to tell their story *one more time*, who need the freedom to cry without public disdain. I can inspire and encourage others by sharing my personal experiences of failure and, ultimately, success.

Thinking back, there were so many negative events that could have successfully overtaken me and precluded the myriad ministerial opportunities I have had over the last two decades, as well as those I have yet to experience. Had I walked away from my calling when times were tough, I would be wounded and without purpose today. I have to give the glory to God who would not allow me to call it quits when I so desperately wanted to. Instead, God gave me beauty for ashes, the oil of joy for my sorrows, and a coat of praise for my heavy heart. I received godly strength to overcome my deepest hurts, and experienced divine faithfulness in the midst of my doubts and double-mindedness. I am much stronger now than I was at the onset of this journey, which is a direct result of weathering the storms of life and ministry. God knew this would be the outcome and ordered my steps accordingly.

Twenty-two years ago, I had absolutely no idea what I was signing up for when God called me to preach. But, I am so glad I said, "Yes!"

Sage Wisdom *from*

Traditional Pastors

3 ❧ A CLEAR TRUMPET SOUND

Linda H. Hollies

United Methodist Church

Our world, so worn and weary,
needs music, pure and strong,
to hush the jangle and discords
of sorrow, pain, and wrong.
Music to soothe all its sorrow,
till war and crime shall cease
and the hearts of all grown tender
girdle the world with peace.

—Frances E. W. Harper,
"Song for the People"

Once upon a time there was an island whose people lived in the ancient ways. The most prized possession was a conch shell that was sounded ritually to still the winds, to ease the storms, and to placate the rain and thunder beings. It was the islanders' way of singing to the gods. It was a great whorled shell the color of the moon. It was patterned and perfect and well worn. It was entrusted to one family, whose youngest member, whether male or female, guarded it and knew the times to sound the note. It was that one who went out to meet the sea and storms, give the clear conch sound and save the people and the island from destruction as the raging tempests approached.

While in the care of one young man, the shell was carelessly lost. He was desperate and fearful. So he sought to cover his failure. He found another shell, almost identical. After all, he thought, no one will notice, no one will ever know. Eventually a storm approached and he went to the appointed place and sounded the note. The conch shell was to sing to the forces of the approaching elements. The conch shell was to calm, appease, and placate the forces of the sea. Standing high on a crag, overlooking the fierce waters, he blew on the conch shell, but the rain and the thunder beings knew the difference in the sound. They were not calmed by the false note.

The shell was a sacramental storm wall. The shell had been made by the elements, by the very gods of the waters themselves. It had power only as long as the covenant was honored. Without due veneration, without proper respect and diligent care, the covenant was shattered. The ritual alone was not enough. The young man blew a false note and the raging storm came battering in.

The winds and torrents of the raging water swept the young man off the cliff, dragging him down against the rocks and spitting him into an underground cave. Gasping for air and in pain from his wounds, he dragged himself onto a ledge. He was alive, but barely. The cave started to fill with water and the sounds of the crashing of the waves and the moaning of the winds. The ancient music of thunder and lightening was all around him. Deep down in the cavern, the elements came together and spoke to the young man about his deception and fraudulent behavior. Because of him and his carelessness, the whole island would have to be destroyed.

The young man begged for his people to be spared. He confessed that it was his sin, not theirs. His prayer was answered. The gods were appeased to a point. But he had to pay the full penalty. He was to become the full penance and the absolute price. His life had to be forfeited in order to restore the balance. Acknowledging his willful carelessness, he willingly submitted to this plan of salvation.

The music of swirling and rushing waters continued to rise in the cave, forcing him toward the ceiling. He knew that he would surely die. But the symphonic forces promised him that there would be a new covenant established. So, even as he died, he was not lost. For the people of the island had seen him swept from the cliff into the sea. At the instant of his death, the storm subsided. They realized that he had given his life to save them. So he was not forgotten. He lives on in the memory of the people. The very mention of his name is music to their ears.

Time passed and that young man's body was broken down by the elements to bones, sand, shards, and pieces. After a long, long time, another young boy, out fishing in a boat, hauled in a net of fish and brought up a bone, moon white and smooth as silk. He fingered it in awe, lifted it to his lips and blew into it. One note, pure and lasting, was released, loose into the air. At that moment the dead young man's spirit was freed. The ritual continues. For we know that there is music in the air! Music is a key component of the message. Music is the primary median of expression in the black community. Music is art. Music is worship. Music is the living Word of God, alive, moving, pulsating through every beat of our hearts. Music has to be the original form of praise. The conch shell sings. The wind howls. The water ripples. The birds harmonize. The bee buzzes. The mosquito whines. The flowers pulsate in aromatic praise. The rain has the sound of drip-drops. The snow falls in a quiet hush. Hens cackle. Roosters crow. Cows moo. Dogs bark. Cats meow. Hogs grunt. Squirrels make the sound of chitter-chatter. Sheep baa. Hammers ping. Saws zing. Generators hum. Fans purr. For the whole wide world is alive with music. And, we, the music makers, the musicians, the Levites of the tribe, we are called to pitch our one note with a clear and clarion sound.

What happens to the church when we, preachers and musicians, forget the right note? What happens to our people when we allow the raging storms to howl, the waters of tempest to blow while we merrily play the wrong note? What happens to our communities when the discordant sounds we offer do not still, quiet, calm, or appease the angry elements that seek to destroy us? What happens to the black church when the music is so irrelevant that a young rap group, Arrested Development, begins to sing, "We are fishing for religion"? Has the conch shell in the black church been carelessly lost? Who is responsible for the devastation in our neighborhoods? Preachers? Ministers of music? Could it be our fault that with careless, unconnected, and discordant music, the whole black community is being caught up, tossed around and about so that it can be swept away? Even the Holy Scriptures question us: "If the trumpet does not sound a clear call, who will get ready for the battle?" (1 Cor. 14: 8 NIV).

This is a clarion call to serious planning in pastoral ministry. This is a clarion call to engaging scripture to see what it says to us about the music for any given Sunday. This is a clarion call to all of us in worship planning to be more effectively working as a team to design themes around which to build the body of music that surrounds the message and will provide deeper impact to those sitting in the pews. Musicians are the Levites of the church. The priest and the Levites must work hand in hand. It is required of good, competent, capable, and *ministering* musicians that they know beforehand what scriptures will be utilized in order that the music and the Word coincide and call out a clear call for the battles each of us will wage all week. For the battles are fierce at our jobs, in our homes, and in our violent world. Our job is to call out a clear call to battle.

Sisters, we are engaged in spiritual warfare. Worship is not some weekly ritual where we come to feel good, eat a happy meal, and go home. The storms are raging in our life. The seas are fierce in our life. The enemy is beating up on us. The demons of division, depression, and defeat are messing with our minds. The "issues" of our lives have us eating Prozac, drinking Crown Royal straight, no chaser, and considering how to jump out of basement windows to end it all! Now, since the devil is messing with you and with me, why is it that we feel that on Sunday we can coordinate music to make the congregation "feel" good, but not give them the ammunition that they need to return home to the battle, which is continuing every day God sends? We are stormy weather people. We cannot sing sunshine songs all the time. We are forced to engage folks where they live. For the Living Word speaks not only to us, but the Word speaks directly about us.

God's Word is contemporary. It's not simply some nice, ancient document that we blow the dust off of for revival and leave closed up the rest of the year. It's not enough for us to sleep during the message and wake up in time to drop our tip into the offering plate before the benediction! Too many sermons start off in one direction and end up somewhere totally different. That's why it's important— no, it's essential—that the songs and the words of the text meet and match. For if the preacher doesn't "say it," then the choir needs to "sing it"! When the preacher and the choir are in synch, the people can get the message. We need to read the scripture's message, sing the scripture's message, and pray the scripture's message in the words of the song. When young people hear scripture set to music, they can both relate and remember. For we are folks who need to hear the message. And, for us, the message has to be put to music.

Where is the real conch shell? We have been careless along the way. We have neglected—with all our recent technology, with all of our purpose driven models, and with all of our megachurch designs—to keep the music authentic, real, and relating to the scriptures. And the forces of this world have noticed that the musical notes, the rituals of prayer, and the preaching sounds within our churches have no power to stop them from their wanton acts of destruction!

"If the trumpet does not sound a clear call, who will get ready for the battle?" "If" is a big word. "If" means suppose this would occur. "If" can change your world! "If" is a word of condition. "If" I had not done this or that. "If" I had not met this person. "If" I had not gone here or there. Circumstances would be different. Situations could have been avoided. Events would not have occurred, "If!" A small two letter word that makes a world of difference. My Granny used to say, "If a bird had a trumpet in it's butt, there would be music in the air!" Granny was a sharp old gal who didn't know about theology, but she knew common sense. We know that birds don't have trumpets. And we know that something is missing as we seek to prepare God's people for spiritual warfare!

I invite you to consider engaging scripture on a regular basis. I know that you engage the scores. I know that you wrestle with words, tunes, and melodies. I know that you have to pull teeth to have folks show up and not cut up and clown as they come to rehearse. But I want to invite you to get serious about reading, and rereading and then allowing the scriptures to read you! Who wrote the passage? What was the purpose of the passage in its context? What are the central themes that the passage is addressing? Which of the themes have universal implications? Who are the central figures? How are they like you? What is the invitation to them in this passage? What are they to do so that life improves? What is the invitation to you? What is the invitation to those who are involved in music ministry with you? What is the "good news?" What word is fresh, alive, and worthy of being proclaimed in song?

Proclamation is more than the word sung, prayed, or spoken! Proclamation includes the ambiance that surrounds the setting in which the drama of God's intervention happens. How is the stage set for this living story to unfold? What does the sanctuary say about the Living Word? How does the altar speak to the message that is to be proclaimed? What are the visual images that can be captured, portrayed, and illustrated in both speech and art?

All that we do is part of the holy act of lifting high the incarnate and Living Word who is Jesus Christ. People come because they are seeking a fresh word, a now word, and a word that can provide them both help and hope for the coming week. People come because their fuel has run low, their hopes have dissipated, and their dreams are fading fast. And, since the Bible plays a supremely authoritative role in the church community, you and I must probe, examine, and search the Scriptures in order to help those in the pew discern God's continuing actions, activities, and intervention in our world.

One of the tools that I find so helpful in keeping me grounded is called the common lectionary. Lections or passages of scripture are taken from the Hebrew text, the Psalter, a Gospel lesson, and an epistle. The Hebrew text or Old Testament is the start of our consideration. The psalm is a reflection based on the Hebrew text. The New Testament lesson and the epistle continue the theme set forth under the Law, before Grace and Truth. There is a tie, a thread, and a common theme that runs between all four texts. The lectionary forces us to struggle with what God is yet trying to tell us. By using the lectionary, preachers are prevented from "mounting their one theological hobby horse" every week. By using the lectionary, we are forced to grapple with unfamiliar and often unpopular scripture texts. We have to work with the conflicts that are part of the church. And the lectionary gives us an overview of biblical unity that is often missing in the black church. The lectionary offers us a framework for worship and preaching the Christian year.

The Christian year begins with Advent. Coming right after Thanksgiving, Advent forces us to prepare our hearts to be the manger for the coming Christ. Advent means "the Coming." Christmas does not show up unannounced! Mary is told she will get pregnant. Advent means that Mary is pregnant. And each of us must make ourselves prepared for the new infant who is due. For several weeks before Christmas and all the festivities of this Holy Day, the lectionary compels us to rethink the reason for the season. The lectionary and the Christian year reminds us that—black, white, Catholic, Baptist, United Methodist, or AME—all of us read the Scriptures. At a most primary level, following the lectionary and the Christian year keeps us in touch with the world of our neighbors, our coworkers and others in the small world village. Lutherans, Episcopalians, Presbyterians, United Methodists, and Roman Catholics have engaged the Revised Common Lectionary to divide the Bible over a three-year period known as A, B, and C.

Year A focuses on the good news found in the book of Matthew. Year B holds the sacred writings of Mark and John. Year C's focus is the evangelist, Luke.

The world is splintered enough, and the common lectionary and the Christian year promote a type of ecumenical unity that follows us from worship into the world. In 1983, the Consultation on Common Texts invited denominations to try their suggestions of a set of lections or common texts that all could use. Each denomination was asked to offer suggestions, amendments, and modifications. The final draft was issued in December of 1991. The intent of the lectionary is to provide sections of scriptures that are arranged according to the Christian year and carry the central message of the Bible, which is Jesus Christ. Lectionaries are not designed to limit the preacher's message or restrict the flow of the Holy Spirit. On the contrary, denominations that use the lectionary find themselves stretched in new and surprising ways, because the scriptures are in synch with contemporary life.

For me the lectionary is a safe tool. As a woman, and African American at that, it is good for me to have the lectionary to call out the hard and difficult word that many congregations don't want to hear. If I call on the text of my own accord, it can be said that "she is beating up on us." What I have done for the past several years is to include the page of scriptures from the worship planner in the bulletin. The worship planner is an idea that any one of you can cultivate for your particular denomination. It lists the four texts on one page. On the other page there are listed suggested hymns, anthems, prayers, calls to worship, and benedictions. If you decide that is more work than you're ready for, simply stop by the book store and purchase a copy of *A Trumpet For Zion: Worship Resource, Year A.* You will discover one full year of all that you need, minus the hymns and anthems. But as you sit with, read, and work with the passages of scripture, the music will arise from within your own soul. For I heard Minister James Moore early in the morning hours saying that he asked God to give him songs to help people make it through the night! This is our ministry, to put the scriptures message to music!

I am not pushing the use of the lectionary. I am pushing a systematic approach to worship planning that coincides with what the wider community, the larger society, may be hearing in worship.

Community groups, family groups, cell groups, and work groups can all talk a common language when we follow the central themes of the Christian year. So, the common lectionary may not be your cup of tea. However, the Christian year will provide us with a general background around which we can prepare our clear and clarion call through music, which will uplift and celebrate scriptures, which will feed us all week long.

The Christian church year begins with the life of Christ. Starting over, fresh starts, and new beginnings are all necessary themes in our communities. There are four Sundays in Advent. Altar, banner, and parament colors (the cloths draping the pulpit, lectern, and altar) are either purple or blue. There is Christmas Eve, which is the water rupturing and labor beginning. And there is Christmas Day or the Nativity of our Lord. We celebrate this world event for the next two Sundays in what is called the Christmas Season. The colors of the season are white, accented with gold.

Epiphany is the season when the church is out and about trying to get a glimpse of Christ in the world. Epiphany is one of the most ancient liturgical celebrations of the Christian church. The actual date is January 6, a couple weeks following the winter solstice, when the sun god was honored as the days began to lengthen. Originally, Epiphany commemorated both the birth and the baptism of our Lord Jesus. "Epiphany" means "manifestation." This means that the Incarnate Son of God has become visible as the Light of the world. God's redemptive purpose can be clearly seen, dispelling the myths, the ignorance, and the folly of sin. Of course, this is the season where we wait for the magi, the wise men, those traveling Gentiles, to make it to the place where the child was with his parents. They came to represent the whole world before this Jewish King.

Epiphany has a strong missionary thrust to it. God sent Jesus. We are sent into the world. Epiphany is the transportation from a particular Jewish community/salvation to a world salvation where all will bow before the King of Glory at the second Advent. God provided light. Jesus is the light. We are to be transparent so that light can be visible in us. The prophet Isaiah gave universal prophecies of Gentiles coming to the light of Israel's God. We have arrived. Epiphany reminds us that it is our time to go into the entire world. We continue the ministry of world mission, local mission, ministry to the disabled and disadvantaged. We are known for our ministry to the poor, the hungry, and the illiterate. Epiphany is a good time to remind us of our mission as the people of the Living Christ.

The last Sunday of the Epiphany season is Transfiguration Sunday, where the power, majesty, and dominion of Christ was displayed in trinitarian effects before the disciples on the mountain. The color white is to symbolize light, brightness, knowledge, and joy as we are called to grow in faith and knowledge of the One who came from heaven to earth to save us and offer unto us eternal life.

From transfiguration we are carried to Ash Wednesday and the beginning of the Lenten season of repentance and remembering that we are simply creatures of dust before the Almighty God. There are five Sundays, followed by Palm Sunday and Holy Week. The sanctuary colors are purple. Palm Sunday's color is scarlet. On Maundy Thursday, Good Friday, and Holy Saturday the altar is bare with no paraments to signify the overwhelming grief of the world as the Sacred Lamb is slain. As we spiritually prepare our hearts for Christmas with Advent, so we are made ready for the high holiday of Easter with Lent and its observances of sacrifice, prayer, and watching how the drama of betrayal falls within our realm. Judas is not the only one who betrayed Jesus. One of us lost the conch shell! Lent sends us on a serious search for authentic relationship, holy living, and the mystery of the cross.

First-century Christians observed the forty hours when Jesus was entombed. By the third century the entire week that we know as Holy Week had become the norm. The Stations of the Cross were made available for those who no longer could make the pilgrimage to Jerusalem. Today we observe a tithe of the whole year as Lent. There are actually thirty-six days in Lent, plus Wednesday to Saturday of Holy Week. No Sundays are included in Lent. For every Sunday is an Easter reminder of the power of the resurrection. We are an Easter people. Rising is our constant theme of praise. Consequently, we announce the Sundays in Lent, not the Sundays of Lent.

Palm Sunday marks the triumphal entry of Jesus into Jerusalem. Monday Jesus cleanses the temple. Tuesday there is the discourse on the Mount of Olives where Jesus teaches about the sheep and the goats being separated by God. On Wednesday, Judas agrees to betray Jesus. On Thursday, there is the Last Supper in the upper room. Friday, Jesus willingly goes to Calvary. And on Saturday the tomb is sealed with a huge stone. But Sunday comes!

Easter is the highest day of praise in the Christian church, for Jesus conquers sin, death, and hell! The Easter Season consists of seven Sundays, which shows us the formation of the early Christian Church. Easter colors are white and gold; the rest of the season is white. The Easter Season carries us toward the birthday of the church, which is Pentecost, when the Holy Spirit comes with *dunamis* power, which gives us victory over sin! This is a day when the color is red to signify the flames that sat atop each one present in the upper room.

Pentecost (*pentecoste*) is the Greek word for fifty. This Sunday signifies the fiftieth day after the resurrection. This historical event is recorded in Acts, chapter 2, as the Holy Spirit descends upon the church gathered in the upper room. This is the promise of the Christ for their power, their strength, their guide, their comfort as they "Go into all the world and make disciples." The resurrection, the ascension, and Pentecost are all related and yet very distinctly different. The receiving of the Holy Spirit makes Pentecost one of the major celebrations of the Christian church. For without the bestowal of this great and precious gift, the church could not have been born. Remember! This was the same group who had sat in the room with the windows barred and the doors shut tight, afraid of their fate when Jesus came and spoke "Peace be with you." The Holy Spirit is not some intangible, invisible "being" to be relegated to the background of our lives. It is the power of the Holy Spirit that makes us bold enough to call ourselves ministers of the Word of Jesus Christ. It is the power of the Holy Spirit at work now since we have been so careless with our "conch shells" and clarion call.

The Roman Catholic Church names the balance of the church year "ordinary time." Following Pentecost, there are no major festivals or holy days until All Saints Sunday and Christ the King Sunday, which follows Thanksgiving and precedes Advent. The liturgical color for twenty-five to twenty-six weeks of ordinary time is green for the growth that is expected and anticipated even without the celebrations and festivities we so love.

The lectionary makes clear that, as Christians, we live in the world, but it is not our home! With the gift of a cross-section of scriptures we find ourselves more involved with *kairos* time, which belongs to God and the realm of mystery we call the church universal. Following the church year, we can move back and forth from *kairos* time to *chronos* time—to merely marking chronological dates with ease. Our concept of time and eternity becomes more sharply focused and begins to revolve around the Incarnate Word, Jesus Christ. Using the lectionary and becoming familiar with the church year helps to order our lives with his life, his mission and ministry, his death, and his resurrection. It will keep us looking for the "correct" conch shell! It will force us to keep it pitched correctly! We will begin to watch the storms of life ease! We will see victory and shalom in the earth! For God recognizes the clarion sound of the trumpet. And when we teach them, so will the people we minister to in the pews!

4 ᴄᴧᴜ CREATING BEAUTY FOR GOD

Joyce E. Wallace

United Methodist Church

Our ancestors were able to survive the ordeal of slavery and the Jim Crow years because they carried within them a set of what we call "life-enhancing beliefs" which could not be destroyed. Existing alongside the anti-intimacy messages formed during slavery, these beneficial messages are the jewels of our slave legacy. Tunnel deep into our souls, and they can be found in abundance. When first extracted, some may look dull from disuse, but once polished they have the power to reflect the greatest light. Most of us have always known these beliefs existed; our parents and grandparents often exhibited them in flashes of brilliance. It is now our turn to call forth all of these positive beliefs so that we can create the lives we desire, and attract and maintain love.

> —Brenda Lane Richardson, aka Dr. Brenda Wade,
> *What Mama Couldn't Tell Us about Love: Healing the*
> *Emotional Legacy of Racism by Celebrating our Light*

Our God is a multidimensional, multifaceted God! God is love, but also desire. God is sweet, but also succulent. God is calming, but also rousing. God is simplistic, but also complicated. God is solemn, but also colorful.

Because God is multidimensional and multifaceted, God touches all the senses of our being—what we hear, what we feel, and what we see. Therefore, we not only experience God through prayer, praise, and preaching; we experience God through our emotions, our spirit, and our sight. It is to the latter that this chapter is addressed.

If "what you see is what you get" then it is mandatory that the space set aside for worship speaks out about God's realm, God's power, and God's glory. What is God's realm like?

31

The wall was made of jasper, and the city of pure gold, as pure as glass. The foundations of the city walls were decorated with every kind of precious stone. The first foundation was jasper, the second sapphire, the third chalcedony, the fourth emerald, the fifth sardonyx, the sixth carnelian, the seventh chrysolite, the eighth beryl, the ninth topaz, the tenth chrysoprase, the eleventh jacinth, and the twelfth amethyst. The twelve gates were twelve pearls, each gate made of a single pearl. The great street of the city was of pure gold, like transparent glass. (Rev. 21:18–21 NIV)

In other words, God's realm displays God's beauty, grandeur, and opulence. God's realm is full of color and textures and pizzazz. When we read this description in Revelation, we are stirred, delighted, and impressed. When we read this description it reminds us of a multi-hued, warm, and expressive people often given to glitter and glitz, magnanimity and graciousness. This is what I feel is desirable for our worship spaces.

During my first year of appointment in a new community of many beautiful church buildings, there was one in particular I would pass by regularly and admire. In this city of wonderful ecclesiastic edifices, one was touted among the best and was attended by the landed gentry of a growing southern city. It sat grandly on the corner of a major thoroughfare in shimmering white pristine beauty with high steeples, a bell tower, tall and wide multipaned windows, and precisely manicured lawns.

I wanted to see the inside, which I imagined to be of exquisite beauty. I didn't imagine I would ever get to see the inside of this church, but not only did I get to see the inside of this church, I was invited to preach there. When I entered the chancel of this church from the side door, took my seat, and allowed my gaze to travel down the long center aisle taking in those majestic windows on both sides of the nave, I was disappointed and left cold. Where was all the beauty I had imagined and anticipated?

The walls and ceiling were white; the carpet, draperies, and pew cushions were blue, and with the exception of the wood tones there was no other color. There were no banners hung between the windows; in fact there was none of the warmth of the spirit of the living God displayed. I began to ask myself questions: "How do they worship in a place so devoid of emotional feeling?" "Whom or what do they worship that has so little life?" "Where is the graciousness of God the Creator displayed, the warmth of the love demonstrated by the crucified/ resurrected Jesus?" "Where is the fire and passion of the Holy Spirit sustainer?" "Where is the joy, excitement, and outward manifestation of the inward stirrings that come as a result of giving oneself to Christ and being made new?" Being touched by God is not just a blue and white experience. It is a royal purple, a passion red, a glittering gold, and a life giving green experience. And that is what is needed to create a prayerful, praising, emotionally stirring space in which people come to worship.

When using flowers at all, I prefer live flowers because they are symbolic of life and growth. Live flowers on the altar remind us that God is Creator of all living things and that creation began with the earth and its dressing of grass, trees, and flowers. Artificial plants and flowers are used in many instances due to convenience and cost; however, they don't best represent God.

The church in its primary sense is "the assembly of all believers among whom the Gospel is preached in its purity and the holy Sacraments are administered according to the Gospel." This means that, above all other things, the church is people, believers, who hear the gospel and use the sacraments according to Christ's institution. With this understanding it is possible to say that it does not make a difference where these believers hear the gospel and use the sacraments, whether it be in a traditional church building, a gymnasium, or even a business place.

On the other hand, the place where believers meet is important. After all, the church is also the assembly of people who hear the gospel and use the sacraments. Those people must assemble somewhere, and the character and purpose of their assembly require that the place of the assembly be appropriate for what is going on. Likewise, the place where God's Word is heard and the sacraments received should be in a setting that is conducive to that hearing and receiving and does not detract from it in any way.

The most important reason, however, for being concerned about where God's people are gathered is not because the nature of worship is corporate but because it is sacramental.

Where the gospel is rightly preached and the sacraments administered according to Christ's institution, there God has promised to be. This means that the place of worship is not just symbolic of God's presence but is the place where God is actually present. That God is present demands the utmost of respect and reverence, as Moses experienced in the wilderness: "Take off your sandals, for the place where you are standing is holy ground" (Exod. 3:5 NIV). Accordingly, our churches today need to be shown that respect and, in turn, further that spirit of reverence.

The use of flowers is one type of decorating that is common in many churches. Flowers serve no liturgical function but help to set the mood or tone of an event, as they do when used in our homes. The basic symbolic value of flowers is joyfulness, and as such they are an expression of the goodness and beauty of creation.

When employing flowers as decoration, the first matter that must be kept in mind is the type of floral arrangement. Are the flowers to be cut, or may we use potted plants? Remember that the rule of thumb is that the flowers are to be live. This rule conforms to the principle that objects used in the house of God should be genuine. If one wishes to be consistent with the genuineness principle, then one should demand, for example, that all fabrics and carpeting used not be synthetic nor contain synthetic materials, or that all woodwork be solid and not veneer.

This environment of congregational worship seems bare if it is not somehow adorned for worship—decorated so as to look festive, or somber, or whatever is appropriate to worship on a particular occasion. The ancient Jews richly adorned the temple in Jerusalem, and as soon as the early Christians were able to set aside space especially for worship they began to "vest" this space. The verb "to vest" comes from the Latin word *vestire*, which means to clothe for the purpose of exhibiting authority. To vest the space or furnishings used for worship means to clothe them with material that signifies their holy function.

There is no one and only correct way to vest a Christian place of worship, no authority that has made rules that we must follow. As you go from church to church and denomination to denomination you will see a wide variety of styles. There is much room for the exercise of creativity and imagination. On the other hand, there are ancient traditions that tie us with Christians of many times and places, and there is a growing consensus in many denominations that helps us adapt these ancient traditions so that we can identify with them today.

Paraments are hangings of fine cloth, traditionally silk, which decorate the altar, the pulpit, and the lectern (if there is one). Their colors signify the day or season of the Christian year, and their symbols represent various aspects of the Christian faith. As such, they are powerful devotional and educational tools, and they have been so used since the sixth century c.e. The four basic colors of paraments are red, white, purple, and green. Other colors may also be appropriate. Suggestions for parament colors follow.

In the early church there was no fixed rule for determining the color for a season or festival. Ordinarily the newest and best paraments and vestments were used for the more important occasions. It was not until the sixteenth century that certain colors were assigned to be used during particular seasons and on certain feast days. Complete standardization of colors was not achieved until the nineteenth century, and this, as the story goes, was due only to the commercial influence of the ecclesiastical supply houses.

In 1570 with the reformed missal of Pope Pius V the common sequence, called "the Roman use," was established. The high festivals of Christmas and Easter were white. The preparatory seasons of Advent and Lent were purple. The penitential days of Ash Wednesday and Good Friday were black. The days of zeal (Pentecost) and the martyrs were red. The other days were green. There is no reason that this usage must be adhered to. The external matter of color falls under the category of a diaspora or matters that are neither right nor wrong.

The following is a list of the standard liturgical colors, describing their significance and use during the church year.

Purple: The color of royalty, but also of sorrow and repentance. Purple is used during the season of Advent, on Ash Wednesday, and during the Lenten season (until after the Maundy Thursday service, if Holy Communion is not celebrated).

Blue: The color of spiritual love, fidelity, anticipation, and hope. Blue has become very popular in recent years as an alternate color for Advent, because since the liturgical revisions of the 1960s, the tenor of the season is one of hope and anticipation of the coming of Christ.

White: The color of eternity, symbolizing perfection, celebration, and joy. White is used for Christmas and its season, Watch Night and New Year's Day, Epiphany and the first Sunday after Epiphany, and the Transfiguration of the Lord. It is also used for Easter and its season, Ascension Day, Trinity Sunday, All Saints Day, and Christ the King Sunday. If Holy Communion is celebrated on Maundy Thursday, the color is white.

Gold: The color of riches and glory. Gold may be used on Christmas Eve, Christmas Day and the first Sunday after Christmas, Watch Night, New Year's Day, Epiphany of the Lord, Easter and its season, and Ascension Day.

Green: The color of life, refreshment, and regeneration. Green is used for the for the season of Epiphany, from the second through the fifth Sundays after the Epiphany, and for the twenty-four Sundays of the season of Pentecost, beginning with the second Sunday after Pentecost.

Red: The color of zeal (fire) symbolizing the Holy Spirit and martyrdom (blood). It is used for Pentecost and as an alternative for Psalm/Passion Sunday and Thanksgiving Day. Inasmuch as red is the color for reformation, it is also appropriate for ordinations and consecrations, evangelistic services, dedications, anniversaries, and homecomings. If a color (other than black) is used at all on Good Friday, the color is red.

Black: The color of mourning, humility, and death. Black is used on Ash Wednesday (as an alternative), and Good Friday (if desired).

It is also important to note that, in employing liturgical colors, it is the season of the church year that determines their use. This means that the color of the day or season is not changed for wedding or funeral services. The only exceptions are for services of ordination, church dedication, and the congregational anniversary, where red is the appropriate color.

DECORATING FOR THE SEASONS

Each season of the church year has its own special emphases and appointments that can be used.

Advent: The traditional color for Advent is purple, marking it more as a penitential season. The optional color for Advent is blue, which according to some better reflects the spirit of anticipation and hope.

Christmas: The color for Christmas and its season is white. White symbolizes divinity, eternity, purity, light, and joy, so this color is most appropriate for celebrating the incarnation of the God who came to redeem humankind.

Epiphany: Like Christmas, the color of the Epiphany and its season is white, the color of divinity, purity, and joy. On the second Sunday after the Epiphany, the paraments may be changed to green, since these Sundays, until the eve of the Transfiguration, are considered by the dominant liturgical tradition to be "ordinary time."

Lent: Lent begins on Ash Wednesday with a call to repentance. The color for Lent is purple, symbolizing sorrow and repentance. For Ash Wednesday, the color used in most traditions is also purple. Many churches choose to use black, the color of mourning, humiliation, and death.

Holy Week: The color for Holy Week begins with purple (the color of royalty, repentance, and sorrow) or red (the color of royalty and passion).

One of the most dramatic and emphatic observances of the week is the stripping of the sanctuary and the draping of the altar and other unmovable sacred objects with black cloth at the end of the Maundy Thursday service.

Easter: The color for Easter is white, symbolizing perfection, celebration, and joy. The alternate color is gold, the color of riches and glory.

Pentecost: The conclusion of the Easter season in Pentecost Sunday. The color of the day is red, symbolizing the passion and warmth of the Holy Spirit.

Time after Pentecost: This period of time is the third division of the church year and comprises about one half of the calendar year. It begins with Trinity Sunday, a celebration of the mystery of God, three in person but united in substance, on the first Sunday after Pentecost. The season culminates with Christ the King Sunday. The color for Trinity Sunday and Christ the King Sunday is white; for the remainder of the Sundays after Pentecost, green is used.

BANNERS

Banners can be used in various ways. They can be hung on poles, carried in the procession, placed in stands during the service, and then carried out in the recession. They can be hung from the ceiling, the balcony, or poles perpendicular to the walls. They can be directly hung on walls and columns. Banners are most effective when they highlight the day or season being celebrated, a special emphasis or a particular event in the church, or some timeless Christian affirmation or theme.

Banners should be in good taste, express some aspect of the Christian gospel, and contribute to the spirit of worship.

It should be understood that no one banner is a permanent fixture in the church but is for use on one or more particular occasions or seasons.

Banners should be simple in design and not attract undue attention.

Most of the best banners do not use words. If words are used, they should be few and subordinate in the overall design.

A banner should be hung properly, centered in its space, and an appropriate size so it is framed by its background.

No banner should hide or distract from the cross or the basic chancel furnishings.

Remember to keep all banners well away from open flames, high intensity lights, or heating or cooling vents.

Do not wrinkle fringes, and be prepared to iron out any wrinkles before using after storage. Do not use a soiled or dingy banner or one that is visibly in need of repair.

Most commonly, the pastor has the final responsibility in the selection and use of banners, as in all else relating to the environment and conduct of congregational worship.

VESTING SACRED SPACES

The following principles should guide a congregation's purchase and use of appointments in the chancel and nave:

1. They should not conflict with the theology of Scripture.
2. They should serve a liturgical purpose.
3. Their symbolism or significance should be clear (this matter may involve some instruction by the pastor or altar guild).
4. Avoid clutter, sensationalism, and sentimentalism.

Key words for vesting sacred spaces include the following:

Clean
Pressed
Tasteful
Coordinated

Supportive of theme/theology (appropriate)
Movement/life
Whites should be white

Nothing should detract from the primary function of the communion table, which is to be the place where Holy Communion is celebrated; everything used on the table should be selected and procured with great care and should be appropriate to its holy purpose. Everything should express to the worshiper the qualities of truth, integrity, sanctification, and purity. Anything that expresses falseness or pretense, or that is gaudy or cheaply ornate, should be avoided.

The principle of integrity is not a matter of rigid rules as to what is "correct," nor does it mean that what is more costly or more beautiful is necessarily better. Often the worth of an article is more to be found in the quality of work and material involved than in the dollars-and-cents cost. A cheaper material that is genuine is more appropriate than an imitation of a more expensive material. We express outwardly, by our use of material things, what we are inwardly.

What we see sometimes "speaks" so loudly that it cancels out what we hear, and the sloppy appearance of the chancel can make it harder to hear the preaching of Christian commitment and consecration. On the other hand, this message is powerfully reinforced when the worshipers see before them visual evidence that there are people who care enough to give their best.

TERMS AND DEFINITIONS

Altar: The most important piece of liturgical furniture and the focal point of the worship space. The altar symbolizes the presence of God. Its function is sacramental and sacrificial. The sacramental function is that it is where God gives the people the gifts of Christ's sacrifice, namely, Holy Communion. The sacrificial function means that it is where the congregation offers its prayer, praise, and thanksgiving in response to God's gifts. The altar may either be fixed to the east wall of the chancel or be freestanding.

Chancel: One of the two main divisions of the worship space. It is the part of the building where the altar is located, that is, on its actual or so-called liturgical east end. In most churches the chancel is one or two steps higher that the nave.

Lectern: A piece of liturgical furniture in addition to the altar, pulpit, and font. It is normally smaller than the pulpit and is located on the opposite side of the chancel on the same line that divides the chancel from the nave. It serves as the place from where the Scriptures are read. In some modern churches there is no lectern, since the pulpit serves as the place where the Scriptures are both read and expounded.

Linens: A word used to designate the white-colored pieces of cloth used in the chancel. Originally these cloths were made of fine linen, but today a number of synthetic materials are available.

Nave: The large, central area of the church building where the congregation gathers for the service. In traditional churches the nave contains several rows of pews from front to back. To the east of the nave is the chancel and to the west is the narthex.

Paraments: Cloth hangings for the furnishings of the chancel that indicate the day or season of the church year by the liturgical colors. Ordinarily they are made of silk, satin, or some other fine material.

Paschal candle: A large candle used on Easter and during its season to indicate that Christ "the Light of the world" is risen from the dead. It is also used in a service for the burial of the dead and for services in which the sacrament of holy baptism is administered, as a reminder that the life of the Christian only has meaning in view of the resurrection of Christ from the dead.

Pulpit: A principal piece of liturgical furniture with the altar and font. The pulpit is the place of the Word. Ordinarily the sermon is preached from the pulpit, but the readings may be read from there as well.

Sanctuary: The part of the chancel where the altar is located. Sometimes it is set off from the choir by an altar rail. In popular usage the term is used to refer to the entire area in which services are held, namely, the chancel and the nave together.

Imagination! Imagination is the key when it comes to vesting the space where we meet God. My prayer is that you always use your imagination to give God glory and honor.

5 ∽ Ministry Lessons Learned from Working with and for Others

Linda Boston

Evangelical Lutheran Church, USA

Worship is an important expression of [a] congregation's self-determined identity. . . . [T]he order of worship printed in the weekly bulletin, for example, illustrates special emphasis and acknowledgment of the movement of the Spirit through its fourfold divisions: "Invoking God's Presence," "Inviting God's Pleasure," "Illuminating God's Word," and "Implementing God's Purpose." Throughout this movement, worship is clearly the embodiment of the Spirit. Following the acolytes, the procession of the choir and pastoral staff takes a back seat to the energy of liturgical dancers moving down the aisle to the beat of drums, organ, and piano. This . . . "is a piece of our cultural and spiritual ancestry that gives a different flavor to the experience of procession and transition within the Invocation. It encourages congregational participation, . . . invokes the full, robust presence of God within the people." It is instructive to note that the pews face the chancel area, which has musical instruments, a podium . . . with choir seated behind, an elevated cross, and a mud-cloth draped altar with candles and Bible. . . . "[T]he altar is [not] insignificant, but . . . the whole (chancel) space is an altar." . . . Rather than a primary focus on a single sacred object, it is an attempt to acknowledge a broader and more embodied and holistic proclamation of the gospel seen in the sacred symbols, the musical instruments, and the celebrants. . . . "[I]t parallels the African notion of a participatory embodied experience with spiritual power and presence."

— Julia Speller, *Walkin' the Talk:*
Keepin' the Faith in Africentric Congregations

Therefore then, since we are surrounded by so great a cloud of witnesses, let us . . . throw aside every . . . unnecessary weight, and that sin which so readily clings to and entangles us, and let us run with patient endurance and steady and active persistence . . . the race that is set before us" (Heb. 12:1 AMP).

Dear sisters: I offer some of my greatest lessons in ministry—the wisdom that I have gained from mistakes, mine and others. And to my dear Sister Angela and all the other sisters like her, my heartfelt and well-learned advice to you is please, please, please learn from the ministry mistakes of others. You can't live long enough to make all the ministry mistakes yourself. Mistakes are inevitable; try as you may not to, you will make them. Acknowledge them, learn from them, ask for forgiveness, and move on in Jesus' name. If for no other reason these life lessons are given to us so we will be invaluable to others to keep them from going down that road at the end of which, having traveled it ourselves, we know awaits a monster, a boogie bear of the highest order.

Recall the lesson from the woman at Simon's house who anointed Jesus' feet with oil—the author names her only as a sinner (Luke 7:36–50). Remember, sister girl, men sin, women sin, we all sin, we all make mistakes, we all fall short of God's glory sometime. By the way, it is Simon who makes the mistakes in this lesson. Simon was into keeping himself and others bound, weighed down by their mistakes. The woman had learned to put past mistakes behind her and move on.

Consider Moses—sins of omission and commission. It wasn't so much what he did as what he didn't do that kept him out of the promised land. In all your learning get understanding.

MINISTRY MISTAKE #1: Letting Mistakes Limit Your Creativity

For I know the thoughts and plans that I have for you, says the Lord, thoughts and plans to prosper you and give you peace, and not for evil, to give you hope in your final outcome. (Jer. 29:11 AMP)

We are far more than our mistakes. The sum of the whole is greater than its parts. We can become immobilized for ministry when we fear repeating mistakes, cease trying for fearing of making a mistake, become paralyzed with self-doubt about making a mistake. Whatever mistakes you make, believe me, somebody else made the same or similar mistake more than once.

Remember the saying: "Nothing beats a failure but a try." It's true. I have discovered that whenever I didn't try something—because I was afraid of the outcome or of hearing, "It's never been done that way around here before"; "That's not going to work"—lunacy happened. We continued to do that same nonproductive thing in the same old way, reaping the same nonproductive results.

My sister, there is something about the power of God's word—believing in it, living by it, standing on it—that is unbeatable. "My Word . . . will not return to me void" (Isa. 55:11 AMP). In my years of living with God, not just doing ministry, but in walking with God, I have discovered that when I focused on Christ, set my face toward Jerusalem, and tried, I sometimes failed and failed miserably, but I always moved forward. What I mean by this is that I learned something new about the situation—about myself, about ministry, about God, about how to solve the problem, whatever it was—through trying, attempting to do something. It was in the doing that I learned the power of Christ found only in mistakes. "My grace is sufficient for you, for power is made perfect in weakness" (2 Cor. 12:9 ESV).

One of the great lessons I learned through making mistakes, and I have made many mistakes, is not to underestimate my own ability and the ability of those around me—those people who are godsends to help you with God's ministry. This brings to mind another mistake.

MINISTRY MISTAKE #2: Believing This Is Your Ministry, Not God's

Remembering this will help you to love and forgive others and yourself when they and you fall short of your godly expectations. But accountability counts; you are accountable to God for the ministry to which God has called you. And if that weren't enough, you are also accountable to that congregation.

Learn to partner with those whom God has not only entrusted to your care but has placed in the ministry to assist you with God's work. Find your inner circle—identify your leaders and cultivate them. Begin to ask, "How do I do this *with* the board—not get it *past* the board?" Learn the rules of being part of a team, even if you are the leader. Work together according to long-range plan; don't forget to have one.

MINISTRY MISTAKE #3: Forgetting to Seek and Receive Wise Counsel

Learn to take wise council from others, in addition to your own. You can't lead until you learn to follow. We can take a lesson from the biblical mentors. Remember the story of Naomi and Ruth. No woman or man is an island. We can't go it alone. We weren't created to go it alone, so don't try to make it on your on. Following the right person is a good thing. Remember, our mistakes, sins, and errors, times when we fall short of God's glory, are not so much allowed for our punishment but as life learning lessons for our ultimate perfection. Recall the lesson from David when the prophet Nathan confronted him with his sin. What was the punishment? What was the lesson? What did David learn from his mistake? What can we learn from his mistakes?

Seek wisdom for your board meetings. Just one word of advice: Make the relationship a loving partnership, not an ongoing hate-filled feud. In your ministry, especially within your leadership circle, create a culture of high trust. Where there is no love, there is no trust. Learn to listen without getting hurt. Learn to hear truth while accepting criticism. Surround yourself with people who will speak the truth to you and listen—make it safe for them to do so. Share the ministry; there is more than enough work for everyone. Learn to share the glory—give credit where credit is due. Even if no one ever says thank you to you, say it to yourself and get on with God's work.

MINISTRY MISTAKE #4: Forgetting to be the Representative of God's Love, or Thinking More of Yourself Than a Child of God Should

Never let your anger give way to rage. For you will see your rage give way to resentment, and resentment to embitterment. And from there it just goes down hill. You begin to dislike, even hate those whom God has given you to feed, nourish, guide, love, and protect. "Simon, son of John, do you love me? . . . tend my sheep. . . . feed my sheep" (John 21:15–17 AMP).

Have I ever lost my temper with others? Yes. Have I thought more highly of myself (or my own opinion) than I should? Yes! Yes! Have I regretted it? Yes. Has the knowledge made me a better person—more aware? Yes.

Have I repeated sins, blunders? Yes. Have I lingered a little too long in the valley of guilt over my mistakes, thus forgetting to love and forgive myself? Do I sometimes grab mistakes and become a victim of my mistakes? Yes. Then it is important to remember that a victim never learns. Do I find myself repeating the same mistakes more or less? Less, as I continue to move toward perfection in Jesus Christ, toward the mark of the high calling in Christ Jesus. Will I reach the goal of total error free perfection? "Not that I have already obtained this or have already reached the goal; but I press on to make it my own, because Christ Jesus has made me his own. Beloved, I do not consider that I have made it my own; but this one thing I do: forgetting what lies behind and straining forward to what lies ahead" (Phil. 3:12, 13).

It is easy as a pastor to remember the wounds that I have received from a wayward sheep or two, or three, or a whole sheepfold full of straying sheep. But when I face myself honestly, then I think of the sheep I have wounded.

Remember—be angry and sin not. Anger is only one letter short of danger. To handle yourself, use your head. To handle others, use your heart. For more ministry advice I commend you to the Scriptures, more specifically to the book of Proverbs. I encourage you to read it and read it often. There you will find such godly wisdom as is condensed in this list:

- Be driven by grace more than truth. Don't sweat the small stuff—and it's all small stuff.

- What we fear we may experience is sometimes greater than real experience.

- Enjoy and embrace your ministry mistakes. Ministry is more about recovery and correcting what you do than being perfect.

- Understand the law of consequences—for every action there is an equal reaction.

- Understand that you can't control as much as you thought or would like.

- Become more comfortable with your real place in life.

- Learn how to play again; have leisure time and idle hours.

- Remember, the down side of ministry is that it never ends.

- Remember, the good side of ministry is that it never ends.

Embrace your mistakes; they will help you become comfortable, at peace, with yourself. Your relationships will reflect it and in your mind there will be a steady outpouring of new ideas.

And now my dear sisters, may God continue to bless you, may God's face continue to shine upon you and give you God's peace. Amen.

Sage Wisdom *for Those*
Entering Ministry Unconventionally

6 ∾ Girl, Just Follow God

Lucille Jackson

African Methodist Episcopal Church

Decisions about love, security, relationships, career, health, family, finances, faith thrust themselves upon our consciousness innumerable times throughout our lives, but haven't you noticed those times when some decisions *feel* different? Thousands of small and large decisions are made in a lifetime, but there are the ones that rise up and catch you by the throat. They scream at you to pay attention. Listen within. What is your heart telling you? You're at a critical intersection in your life, a fork in the road, a shift inside. The planets have lined up; heaven is holding its breath; ancestors are peering over your shoulder; you are staring back at yourself. These are the decisions that touch the essence of you, that make you face up to certain things: What do you want out of your life, how do you feel about yourself, what do you believe about yourself, how much truth can you stand, where do you feel the spirit leading you, what choices are you willing to make in order to become and what sacrifices are you willing to make to go there? Choose. Decide. Risk. Dare. Who will you be? What matters most? No one ever tells us that it's precisely these moments (designed by God) that help us discover who we are inside. They test us, they refine us, they make us, they break us, and then they leave us strong in our broken places. We are forever changed once we face these moments and choose which path we will take.

—Renita J. Weems, *What Matters Most: Ten Living Lessons in Living Passionately from the Song of Solomon*

December 26, 1971, in the basement of my sister and copastor, Rev. Esther Mitchell, we started a church! Neither one of us has a seminary degree. Both of us came through the licensing classes of our denomination in the African Methodist Episcopal Church in the

Illinois Annual Conference. And both of us agreed that God led us to begin a church in the Maywood area. We just decided to follow the voice of God! In May of 2006, we were featured in *Ebony* as sister-clergy friends who have weathered the storms of life, together, over these years.

Esther had begun a Bible study in 1962 after a serious illness, when the physicians gave her up to die! She began a year of serious personal study of the Holy Scriptures for herself. When she completed her year of study, she opened her home to others who wanted a deeper examination. I joined, along with about thirty other folks. Primarily there were women, but a few couples joined, too. We all began to grow in our spiritual development as we learned and worshipped together. Esther heard God say, "Move to another level."

Wisdom is found in the counsel of many, declare the Proverbs. So, as she talked to me and we talked to God in prayer, we decided that the next level had to be a church. Esther is the daughter of a preacher. She had been raised at her father's appointment, Canaan AME, in Maywood. It was a traditional church with traditional teachings. Both of us knew that God wanted us to teach the fullness of the Holy Spirit as AME clergy.

On December 26, 1971, our first worship service was held with a homemade pulpit created by Esther's husband, Jimmie, attended by her three children, James William, Gary Scott, and Dawn Cherisse; Jimmie's mother; my daughter, Paula Ann; my mom, Pauline Ramsey; and several visitors from Canaan. My "baby" sister, Gloria, played the piano for us that Sunday. How the Holy Spirit moved in that basement and Jimmie and our children joined as our first members, along with a church mother. We were excited about doing ministry. We never thought of all the roadblocks that would be set before us in the days to come. We were simply following God.

Anyone familiar with our denomination knows that women in ordained ministry face a difficult time when it comes to "ample" appointments. By "ample" I refer to those where there is a building, some people, and some money to pay our apportioned church fees. I'd been offered a church in the small town of Galesburg, Illinois, but my daughter, Paula Ann, was in school, I didn't drive, had no car anyway, and was working at Malcolm X College as an administrative assistant while trying to complete my undergraduate degree. So, as I prayed mightily about this offer from the presiding elder, I heard God say clearly, "Stay where you are!" I'm a firm one in believing that God knows best, and I followed that voice of direction.

That next year, 1972, we went to present our new church to the Annual Conference. Our bishop, the Rev. Howard Thomas Primm, was a stickler for the rules. He insisted that he would only put one of our names on the appointment. Since we were meeting in Esther's home, I felt it only right and proper to put the appointment in her name. I can't tell you the pain of being "invisible." I can tell you that it was not until the late 1990s that my name was finally added to our appointment! By then, we had completed a more than two-million-dollar building campaign, which resulted in both a church building and an elementary school. Having my name on a piece of paper never stopped me from following God and being copastor of James Memorial Church. But the pain was there.

When Bishop Primm made his final decision and gave Esther the appointment paperwork, he said to us, "Now, you girls go back out to Maywood and do what the Lord said to do." Believe me, we did! By Ash Wednesday of 1972, we had bought a small dentist office in the area, for the neighbors had complained about the traffic that was around the Mitchell's home. By then, God had said that we needed to open a school and do the enrichment education and performing arts education that was missing in public schools. So we did.

Both of us traveled to Pensacola Christian College for a look at their curriculum during the summers. Then we held two years of summer programming for children in our area and the vision of a school unfolded. The dentist office that we had bought had small square footage, but every foot was utilized! Both of us taught, along with several others who could "see" our vision for enriched education for our children. Every Friday night, the school was packed into giant plastic tubs, desks were put in our storage bins outside, and we "unpacked" James Memorial "Church." This went on for years, years, and more years until God said, "Build!"

We knew that it was time to expand. We had grown in membership and many individuals sowed seeds of faith into both the ministry and the school. To each one of them we owe great thanks. My brother, Ramsey Lewis, did marvelous music ministry on our behalf and I'm grateful to my little brother and my sister, Gloria. Dr. Renita Weems, one of our AME clergy sisters, begin to sow into our ministry and to come to Maywood to assist us in preaching and spreading the word of our little school. We began to buy houses that were for sale around us. Then it was time to get a bank loan!

My parents, Ramsey Lewis Sr. and Paulette Richards Lewis, raised me and my two siblings in the aftermath of the Depression. We know about hard times firsthand. My father lost his job, so we lost our home on the south side of Chicago. After much consternation, my Baptist-raised father allowed us to be baptized in the AME Church on the west side, where "Grandma" Bland took us into one bedroom in her home. She was not related to us at all; she was a stewardess at Wayman AME on the north side. All of my parents' furniture, including our piano, had to be put into storage. We all lived in one bedroom off the kitchen. We joined and attended Wayman, where Rev. J. D. Costain was the pastor and the church organist was our first music instructor.

We were black people in a primarily Italian Catholic community. I attended Schiller Elementary School and obtained a first-rate education. What I learned, I put to work as a Sunday school teacher in our local congregation. I was promoted to general superintendent of the department. Esther, meanwhile, was made the district superintendent of the AME Sunday schools. It was here that our lives began this mysterious intersection. Teaching was in our blood. Teaching was a call on our lives. From Esther's Bible school beginnings the Christian education vision grew. We heard God speak. We simply followed God!

My name was not yet on the appointment papers, this many years and this much ministry later. So, as we sought enough money to build both a sanctuary and a performing arts stage, along with an educational center to house kindergarteners to eighth graders, we had a rough time. Banks did not want to grant loans to two women. Finally, without telling her very supportive spouse, Esther was forced to sign a loan from a kindly banker all alone! We learned how to float a bond program, and construction on our building began!

Remember, when you follow God, no one has promised that the way would always be easy. Regardless of whether or not my name was on the paper, Esther and the congregation recognized that I was as responsible as she was for this massive undertaking. Talk about fasting and praying. Talk about staying on our face before God. Talk about being faithful to the disciplines of our denomination. Talk about no help forthcoming from our denomination. Talk about a lonely journey when oftentimes we sought ways where none seemed available. Yet, thanks be to God, we completed our awesome buildings in September of 1981! Talk about a good time, the grand opening celebration was just a foretaste of heaven!

Both Esther and I are approaching the age of retirement. In a few years the bishop will be able to appoint someone else to this ministerial site, for we belong to the AME denomination. Most likely some young man, fresh out of seminary will be sent here as the pastor. Would we do anything differently? Most likely not. We have followed God all the way. Are there regrets and disappointments? Of course there are. Do we have much to celebrate? We have so very much to thank God for in this very present time.

Esther's husband, Jimmie, and their three children are active members of James Memorial. One son, Dr. James William Mitchell, MD, a fine pediatrician, is our church organist. Dawn, first lady of Emmanuel AME, where her spouse, Rev. James Parker, is senior pastor, is now a candidate for licensed ministry within our denomination. The other son, Rev. Gary Scott Mitchell, is owner of an All State Insurance agency. He serves on our ministerial staff and is our church treasurer. My daughter, Paula Ann, is our "nurse" and of course works a second job for pay! I've dedicated my life to this ministry. I don't have a huge retirement package and neither does Esther. God, however, has been faithful to us as we have faithfully served God's people in Maywood and beyond.

Bishop Primm told us to go back to Maywood and to do what God told us to do. This mandate has served us and God's people well. It's these words that we pass as a legacy to any woman who dares to enter ordained ministry. Don't concern yourself about the rules and regulations. Just do what God has called you to do. God will make a way! Both Esther and I are living witnesses! And so is the tangible evidence of the James Memorial African Methodist Episcopal Church, with the names of two women on the cornerstone. Now, run and tell this!

7   Sista, Stay Focused

Essie Clark-George

Christian Methodist Episcopal Church

We've come a long way since we arrived on these shores. Like women in my research, some of us are coping, and some of us aren't. We have a long way to go before the wounds that were inflicted upon us during the passage away from our culture can fully heal. But, we are free.

In many ways, we have very traditional views of the importance of relationships and families. In adapting to the twenty-first century, we need to be prepared to reassess our traditional expectations. We can make whatever changes are necessary, and we can help others who need encouragement. Each time that I doubt that I can overcome my own negative experiences with the way others perceive me as a sexual being, I try to remember my ancestors. I visualize them watching and showing me how to be free, to celebrate my womanhood, and to reach out to others. Most important, I bow my head to only God, find peace within myself each day and count my blessings.

God didn't bring us across the oceans that divide Africa and America to leave us alone. We embody a spirit, a strength, and a resilience that have allowed us not only to survive but to move forward. If you think we've got a long way to go, look how far we've come. As an African American woman, I experience a sense of healing and renewal each day, as I recite this creed: *I believe that what I think and feel about myself, and how I care for and protect my body frees me to love myself as God loves me, to gain the respect that I deserve and to help others do the same.*

—Gail Elizabeth Wyatt, *Stolen Women:
Reclaiming our Sexuality, Taking Back Our Lives*

My best advice to my sister is to never confuse your femininity with the divinity that lives within you! Always keep your word, be steadfast in your ministry, and allow the Jesus in you to shine. The love for the people that you lead will be your greatest gift. If you don't love, you won't take the risk of digging way down into the mess of life's ugliness to discover just what is going on with them! Loving the people of God is essential, so you must stay focused on God.

My ministry really began in my family of origin, in West Pointe, Mississippi. I was the oldest of eight children and had to know how to prepare full meals for my family before I was twelve years old. It was in my family that I learned the pastoral skills of delegation and supervision. My parents both worked, and yet we lived in a four-room shack, trying to survive. Because I was such a "good shepherd" to by siblings, my mother promised me a brand new bedroom suite. I spent one night in my new bed, alone. The next night three other siblings moved in with me! I did say it was a four-room shack. I know the struggle of poverty firsthand.

It was the grace of God that allowed me the opportunity to graduate from high school with no life-changing events. Therefore, I could write to my cousin, who lived in Chicago, and ask her if I could come to live with her, for I wanted a better life than my parents. I wanted a good education and a good job. In the small town where I was born, the possibilities to move ahead were next to nothing. I experienced the urge to leave my family and to explore.

I kept busy in school. I was active in the choir all the way from fifth grade until graduation. God blessed me with the gift of encouraging people through song. I kept score for the girl's basketball team and was captain of my cheerleading squad in my senior year. My family was so proud of me when I walked across that stage at graduation. But I knew that I had to leave home.

Because of my reputation with my family, my cousin allowed me to take the bus to Chicago. I have lived in Chicago ever since.

Through the government's Community and Economic Development Association (CEDA) I was able to get a nursing aide certificate at St. Joseph Hospital. There was one old teacher who would hunt me down periodically to tell me, "You have got to do more with your training." Because of her encouragement, I went on to get my licensed practical nurse (LPN) degree. My plans were to become a registered nurse, but love and marriage intervened!

I joined the Pentecostal Church in Chicago. My church, the Garden of Prayer Church of God in Christ, was later renamed Monument of Faith. Apostle Richard Henton remains the founder and pastor. God had blessed me with a ministry of song and I became a key soloist, youth worker, and fund developer as my pastor traveled, doing crusades. Under the direction of Dr. C. Charles Clency, I joined the Voices of Melody and traveled the nation. It was during this period of my life that I learned to see God in all denominations as we ministered across the miles.

It was a minister, Rev. Leon Clark, who was on the bishop's staff, who got my full attention. I gave up my RN plans and for twelve years became a "stay at home" wife, then mother. My son, Mark, and daughter, Glory, were born, and I enjoyed the lifestyle that my husband afforded us. He spoiled me to excess. I couldn't shop or do any heavy lifting. He bought all of my clothes and told me how to dress. I was too naïve to understand the early signs of abuse—his shutting me down, fencing me in, and controlling me with "love."

Apostle Henton bought an old, empty theater and renovated this property into the current church. My spouse and I came on board to assist him. As my personal evangelism ministry began to increase, Leon began to act more and more "funny." I was able to discern that the "good times" were drawing to an end, so I went to work outside our home. I was hired at Marion Business College with the responsibility of hiring home health aids, nurse's aids, and nurses for temporary staffing positions. It was during this period that I experienced my call to ministry! Leon could not hang, because of his jealousy over my music ministry. He went so far as to ask the choir director to put me out of the choir! The more blessed I became, the more restrictive he became. I know the pain of both mental and verbal abuse. Finally, he threatened to leave us. He went back to New York for a visit to his family and stayed a month. When he returned, I had packed all of his things, and I asked him to leave for good.

Our separation was the start of a new prayer life for me. Going to work at South Shore bank, in the Neighborhood Institute, was such a monetary blessing to a single mom. God placed me in a position to help others, for my job was to train people in the area, develop leads for them to find work, and then send them out, employed. As I look back now, I can more clearly understand that my every step has been ordered by God.

The day came, however, that I needed four hundred dollars to pay a bill. I sent out an urgent request to God and my phone rang almost immediately! When I told my girlfriend about my need, she stated, "I'm bringing it over now." Oh, the power of having a prayer-answering God! It was not too long afterwards that I got a three-hundred-dollar raise and my income tax return! It was a joy to repay my friend's loan.

In 1991, I begin to pastor and entered the ordained ministry track within the Christian Methodist Episcopal (CME) denomination. Simultaneously I enrolled at Northeastern Illinois University to complete my undergraduate degree and enrolled at McCormick Theological Seminary for my M. Div. I also worked full time and became the administrator for a community development pastor, Rev. Al Sampson of Fernwood United Methodist Church. I learned so much about ministry to the poor, the needy, and the outcast from his mentoring. He taught me how to look at the fields, ready for harvest, and to get busy!

It was in 1996 that I received my first pastoral appointment in the CME denomination. I was appointed by the bishop to a burned-out building frame and a storefront church! Yes, you did read my appointment correctly. The first building's gutted frame was all that stood, while the storefront building needed tuck pointing and there was garbage piled high inside. But I accepted the appointment, for "they" were looking for me to cry, whine, complain, and fail! But I looked at those properties with my focus on God. I saw the reality and God gave me a vision. Plus, my background had prepared me for rehabilitation and community development ministry.

I had six members! So I began to call my sister clergy and my friends to come and to stand with me. We rebuilt that church into a beautiful edifice that stands today as a testimony to what God will do when we stay focused. Murchison-Isom CME Church is alive and well today. Along this journey, I began work on my doctorate and used my daily experiences for my thesis: "Stewardship for Fashioning the People of God." I taught and I learned. I learned and I taught. I know what it means to plant my personal seed into fertile ground so that the members can "catch" the vision.

My children grew up and went to college and I remained single until two of my members introduced me to their brother, Roger

George. Roger, an insurance broker, almost five years ago, became the first gentleman of both my heart and the local congregation! Girlfriends from across the country called and visited, petitioning me, "Give me your steps for getting a husband?" All I could tell them was, "I stayed focused on God!"

Roger makes me laugh. Roger is not afraid of me, the ministry, or my pastoral position. Roger understands my theology of stewardship that includes tithing, but so much more. I understand stewardship to include "tending the garden" where I am placed; to do cosmetic enhancement; to produce seed for planting; to cultivate the soil so that it grows, produces, and gives a harvest. Stewardship, for me, grows into my caring for me and for others, as well as the house of God. Roger can beat me giving, and that says a lot.

When Roger came into my life, every extra penny that I made went into Murchison-Isom CME Church. Bishop Dotcy Isom had given me a letter of resolution stating that the denomination would be my cosigners on the loan. I asked for one million dollars and the bank loaned me, on my signature, two hundred sixty thousand. Each month we had to meet a twenty-five-hundred-dollar mortgage note that rose to twenty-eight hundred dollars. We were able to renegotiate the loan down to a more manageable fourteen-hundred-dollar payment. Finally, in 2003 under the leadership of Bishop Paul A. G. C. Stewart, I was able to release all financial responsibility to the Third Episcopal District of the CME Church!

Because I tithe, I have never been concerned about meeting financial obligations. I realize that it's God's responsibility and not mine! So, in August of 2005, when I was appointed as senior pastor of Israel CME, in Gary, Indiana, with a monthly mortgage note of sixty-seven-hundred dollars per month, it was no issue! This landmark congregation had built a new worship center in 1996, and it's a beautiful edifice.

I'm thankful for this opportunity and I'm thankful that my life has taught me much about supervision, delegation, and loving the people of God. I had to come to Israel cleaning up the mess of the former pastor and administrator. It seems that every female pastor that I know has to do "clean up" at some time in her ministry. So be on the look out, and always remember all the life lessons you have learned along the way. My first six months found me having to raise most of the forty-two-hundred-dollar conference claims that were due. I put on a Black Tie Gala and we had glorious fun raising God's money!

Already I can see the vision for Israel within the next five years. Israel will become a complete social service ministry to meet the needs of those in our area. We are housed in an almost abandoned part of the city. We have bought up old, boarded-up houses; we have bought and cleared lots; we have begun a weekly feeding ministry and plan to use community development principles as we "seek the welfare of the city."

Housing developments are in my vision. A referral-based mental health care ministry is in my plan. We have already undertaken two schools to mentor and partner with for the uplifting of our sons and our daughters. My immediate goal is to implement a pastoral care ministry for grief, trauma, and life issues. We are the community of the faithful. Jesus Christ has left us in charge of the hurting and the lost. My journey has not been easy, but all along the way, I'm so thankful that I've kept my focus on God. I urge every sister to do the same! It pays to serve Jesus. It pays every day! It pays every step of the way! I know—for I'm reaping now!

A New Beginning in a New Dimension

Florida T. Morehead

Nondenominational

Beginning anew is not to ask for forgiveness. Beginning anew is to change your mind and heart, to transform the ignorance that brought about wrong actions of body, speech, and mind, . . . and to help cultivate your mind of love.

—Thich Nhat Hanh, *Essential Writings*

Our website boldly states: "Here at Shalom, we have a kingdom assignment to share the Peace of God through Persuading, Equipping, Acting, Celebrating, and Embracing. Shalom is blessed with an anointed pastor, Florida T. Morehead. She is a faithful, fervent servant who is full of love. She shepherds, teaches, preaches, counsels, and administrates in excellence. We here at Shalom are blessed to have a five-star pastor!"

This is not the way that I would dare to introduce myself to anyone, but I followed the call to open the doors of Shalom on my fiftieth birthday! This was not my plan, but the "General" whom we call God had given me marching orders. Being born and reared in the cotton fields of Arkansas, my parents, my siblings, my church, and my community had taught me the virtues of compassion, commitment, and conscientiousness. As a poor family, we were always seeking ways, methods, and strategies to enlarge, elevate, and expand our borders and our territories. I learned at an early age that our God is an awesome God.

My early desire was to become a teacher. I loved math. I was enchanted with the sciences. So I majored in chemistry. Yes, I did! Both my bachelor's and master's of science degrees are in chemistry from the University of Arkansas. I was a chemist—never had a thought about becoming a pastor. Graduated, got a good position at a major chemical company, and, as the young folks say, "Had it going on." Along the way, I got married, had my daughter, Sonya, got a divorce, and joined New Jerusalem Baptist Church in Flint, Michigan. I got way involved in the ministries of Christian education. I was a happy sister in Jesus Christ.

God blessed me to organize a number of different ministries, doing all sorts of things, and I ran into a young woman who was attending the church. Erika came from an abusive home and she seemed to "fit" with Sonya and me. She lived with her aunt, and she was always looking for a family of her own. We began to bond and she starting spending more and more time at our home. Long story, very short, we eventually accepted and adopted her into our family. She has given me my only granddaughter, Iyanna Warren, who is an "active, active" member of our church!

In 1987, the chemical company I worked for "lent" me to the National Society of Black Engineers as their executive director for two years. The company paid my salary, and I lent my expertise and networking skills to this student-led association. I believe that networking and being available to the community are essentials in our world today. I was able to help the organization to acquire a building, and I brought in tons of money, resources, and job placement assistance across the board. After the two years, I left the security of the chemical company and stayed with the students for more than six years. I thought that this was my future. But God called, "New directions."

In my moving, shaking up things, directing students, I began to feel a call to ordained ministry. I quickly shook that off. But I did decide to enroll in seminary and started in a Master's of Divinity program at Howard Seminary in 1988. I completed seminary in May of 1991, while yet working more than full time with the Society. I joined an AME Church in Ft. Washington, Maryland, the same year that I started seminary and became extremely active with responsibilities for young adults, singles, Christian education, media ministry, and as administrator of the music ministry. I was paid, part-time, on the ministerial staff.

The year 1993 was a mile marker for me, as I was near completion of the construction of my home. Things were looking up, The Society was stronger than ever before, and the church was growing faster and larger. Donald Vails, the masterful minister of music at the AME church, was invited to be part of the hoopla around incoming President Bill Clinton's administration. It was my responsibility to get the choir and musicians back and forth for rehearsals and to the performance. I missed part of the board meeting that the students had called.

A short time later, I was called to attend an unscheduled meeting early one Saturday morning and was told that my services to the Society were no longer needed! Talk about being floored! The students said that I was "too busy" for them, with all of my "outside church" activities. Can you say the word "fired"? And I was only about thirty days away from closing on my brand new house! Talk about calling on God, who came through with miracle after miracle.

Networking is essential. Sharing with others the burdens that you carry is essential. Trusting God to work it out and to come through on time is essential. A member of the church, Hazel O'Leary, worked in the U.S. Department of Energy. She offered me a position as a consultant to the Department of Energy. She negotiated a much higher salary that I'd been making. She worked out all the paperwork so that, with my severance pay from the Society, I closed on my house, on time! After three years at the DOE, I decided to start my own business, Shalom Enterprises, Inc. It was a management consulting firm that did events planning and small business development. Life taught me that multiple streams of income are always better than one. When you own your own business, when you can be your own boss, others you work for might determine a salary, but they can never determine your income.

My new house was "da bomb"! I was so proud of what God had allowed me to accomplish as a single mother of two young adult daughters. There was only one small problem with a set of doors, which required a locksmith. The locksmith entered my life to fix the doors. He eventually tried to wreck my life. The signs, the signs, the signs—always be alert to the signs. I ignored the flashing lights. He was a professional locksmith. And he was a black Baptist minister. I met him in 1994. We courted, got engaged, and I married a crazy man in November of 1995.

He had been previously married for a long period and didn't have nor did he "like" kids. His first wife had children who hated him. And, to tell the truth, my daughters didn't care for him either. But, he was a black, saved, professional, preaching man. I forgot the crazy part! In less than six months my home and my life were in turmoil. God called for new directions as I was undergoing tremendous stress in my home and personal life.

About nine months before my fiftieth birthday, I got pregnant with a vision of starting my own church! This was not a physical pregnancy, for the husband's favorite game was to withhold sex! Did I say crazy before? Anyway, with three couples from Ebenezer, my two daughters, my goddaughter, and three single people, we begin to work towards a new church start. In my housing development and surrounding areas, we did questionnaires, we did flyers, and we discovered that people were interested in a nondenominational church. This satisfied me just fine. I had joined the AME system but didn't care for the structure of a bishop telling me what I could not do after God had told me what to do. Plus, I was born and raised Baptist, and I knew that was not an option. So nondenominational it was to be.

We found a community center, Harmony Hall, to rent for our first worship service. With the core group of twelve on February 22, 1998, Shalom Ministries was born. Family and friends flew in from around the country. We had a Saturday night gala and a house full of people. Sunday evening my former pastor from Flint, many members of New Jerusalem and others came for the official installation service. My husband never put in an appearance! I did mention that he was crazy, right?

By September of 1998 the stress and turmoil caught up with me. I had constant pain in my chest. I was on an emotional roller coaster. The husband caused constant havoc and both of my daughters moved out. I had stress tests that showed nothing. But finally I demanded help. An angioplasty showed that I had a 90 percent blockage in the left main artery to my heart. The surgery was that same day. I realized that my husband was the cause of my arteries being blocked, but I tried to maintain the marriage. I'd made a vow before God with a crazy man. I was trying to keep my word.

The church kept growing. My misery kept growing. I loved serving as pastor at Shalom, but my personal life was a mess. I was back and forth to the hospital with heart problems. I have had to have four or five stents put in my arteries. Then, in May of 2002, I had a brain aneurism! God called, "New directions."

After returning from the hospital, I had to move out of my own house. The husband kept up mess, junk, garbage three days straight.

He was trying his best to kill me. His jealousy was out of control. It was jealousy over the growing of Shalom Ministries, not over a man. For in less than ten months, we had more than a hundred members and needed to find our own place. After the third altercation in three days, I had to make a hard decision. I moved into the home of one of my daughters and later filed for divorce! I had to sell my home for the sake of my life and freedom. The ex-husband got half the proceeds! But it was easy to let go of what had become a nightmare from hell. The divorce was granted in July 2003. God promised me double for my troubles! I stepped on in faith.

At ten months old, Shalom Ministries begin to look for more space to rent or to lease. We had no idea of purchasing, just looking for more space. A realtor from the AME church was helping us to seek possibilities. She told me about a small strip mall that had gone into foreclosure. It was just over eleven thousand square feet, and the asking price was five-hundred twenty-five thousand dollars! When we took the tour, I heard God say, "This is it!" I begin to "see" where the sanctuary would be, how the chancel would look, and where classrooms and my office could be located. We had a building; now we needed finances.

We prepared the paperwork. We shopped from bank to bank. We were turned down by all of them. But I was a member of the Collective Banking Group that was formed by a group of pastors. In my networking mode, I called and asked for a face-to-face meeting with Mr. Sandy Fitzhugh, who said to me and his backers, "We will make this happen!" I took a leap of faith. They took a leap of faith. God had put the right people in place, at the right time, with the right resources to help us accomplish the work God had placed before me.

We borrowed four hundred fifty thousand for the mortgage, plus another fifty thousand for the renovation. On Palm Sunday of 1999, Shalom Ministries Christian Center members marched around that building in celebration, claiming the victory in God. By May, we went to closing, and, had our first worship in our new home in September 1999! The dedication service was held that October with Bishop Alfred Owens of Mt. Calvary Holy Church of America presiding. We have come under Mt. Calvary's ministry as a covering and for accountability and fellowship.

I invite you to visit our website at www.shalomministries.biz. I invite you to come and visit us in worship. We are a busy church on the side of the road making impact to advance the God realm. We established a preschool, a before and after school program, and a Saturday academy to assist our youth with academic, social, and cultural skills. I completed my DMin., using Shalom as my area of study, with all of the counseling methods that our congregations require to be healthy in their functions.

Through it all, God has been great, gracious, and generous to me and to Shalom. I have had my challenges. I have had my pain. I have had my heartaches. God has kept me through it all. I am an adjunct professor at the National Bible College and Seminary. I teach classes in pastoral care and counseling. I serve as department chair for evangelism, for people need Jesus in their lives.

God has sent me so many wonderful people to assist in the ministries of Shalom. I have a wonderful male assistant pastor, Elder Jeffery A. Chandler, who also serves as our church administrator. I have three associate pastors, one male and two females. I have a ministerial staff of six women and two men. Ericka, my daughter, is one of them. My administrative assistant is female and the operations manager is a female. Our people are loving, caring, warm, generous, tithing, helpful, worshipping, family oriented, praising, and competent members. The members of Shalom call me a five-star pastor. I call them ten-star people! They treat me like royalty. I'm cared for, cared about, thought about, and generously loved and appreciated.

I almost forgot to tell you: I built a bigger, more gorgeous home! My daughters bought me a cute little dog that I named Angel. And I can count on my granddaughter Iyanna coming to spend the night in "her" room!

What more can I tell you? I'd say, listen to God! Don't hear or follow the voices of others. Be bold. Take steps of faith. Trust God's plan and purpose, and allow God to orchestrate the events of your life. And always pay close attention to the signs! Our anointing will attract many folks, good-looking men included. But, Sista, heed the signs, and listen for God to call your orders for new beginnings and new directions! I bless you on your journey.

Veneese V. Chandler

Pentecostal Assemblies of the World

Straight talk about the loves and troubles of our bodies is almost impossible because there is so much pain. Paradoxes become apparent in very strange ways. Recently, when speaking at a conference, I pointed out the ways in which we needed to engage in ministry that addressed the ways in which the culture responded differentially to little girls who were considered "pretty" and those who were considered "ugly." This "pretty"/"ugly" dichotomy is so taken for granted within Black culture that it is almost never discussed. Girls not considered beautiful by white American standards, if they are part of families and communities who take education and achievement seriously, are groomed to be good students and to be leaders. The others may also be groomed that way, but unless they grow up in middle-class settings where certain protections are in place, they walk a very treacherous pathway to adulthood that may leave them educationally and professionally underdeveloped and very vulnerable targets for all sorts of sexual aggression and exploitation. The failures of African Americans to address this problem is evident in the sad and sorry history of Black women in beauty pageants.

—Cheryl Townsend Gilkes, *If It Wasn't for the Woman*

I believe, to the seat of my sanctified soul, that the very kernel of my ministry and yours begins as we seek to look into, check out, and discover the reasons for our own craziness! There is something within us that seeks to be free of the pain that haunts us and causes our walking woundedness that lives in us every day. And I can tell you from firsthand experience about family dysfunction and physical, emotional, and verbal abuse.

Of course I had no knowledge, as a child, of what caused my mother to be so abrasive. As the youngest of three children, I thought that she was angry with me. Today, with psychological awareness, I would diagnose that my mother was bi-polar with bouts of schizophrenia, exacerbated by a chronic heart disease. She drove both my older sister and brother away from home with her extreme behaviors. I was raised almost as an only child, on the west side of Chicago, in extreme poverty.

My mother, Lillian Arnold Rance, was a white–dress wearing member of Faith Temple COGIC (Church of God in Christ), where I was raised. Her behaviors and mood swings did not give me a "pretty picture" of salvation, but I developed a serious prayer life before age eleven, trying to survive the craziness in my home and the pain in my spirit. I gave my heart to Jesus Christ and clearly remember and honor our pastor, Bishop H. W. Goldsberry, who was a pastor-teacher who encouraged me and my continuing education efforts.

The school and public libraries were places of refuge for me, allowing me time away from home, where I could "travel" the world, reading the classics. I was shy, but my single mother was always hearing voices that told her things that I was doing. I would be beat for nothing, for no explanation was ever acceptable. I never heard an encouraging word, but my mother was insistent that "You are going to college!" I dared not refuse. Mom had always wanted to be a nurse, but got married and had children instead. She moved from her hometown in Pittsburgh, following her spouse. She and my father, Valliant Vernon Chandler, never married, and I believe that much of her nasty attitude toward me stemmed from her pain of rejection.

It is a fact that I was *never* advised by a high school teacher or counselor to prepare for college! I was black. I was poor. Therefore, at Calumet High School I was told to prepare myself for office occupations, and I did. By age fifteen, I was working in accounts payable at Wiebolt's Department Store and helping us to survive the month past the short welfare checks that Mama received. We never owned a car, but bus transportation was sufficient for all of our needs. Looking back, I had a difficult life, with no help but from God.

Planning to go to college with no assistance helped me to fully trust God. I'm a first-generation college student in my family, and it was the grace of God that got me enrolled. Right before high school graduation I applied for and received a $563.00 grant award from the Illinois Student Grant Program. With my mother being so ill, I decided to take that grant and enroll at Central YMCA Community College and continue to work. You might have guessed that I decided to major in psychology! I wanted answers and freedom from my mental and emotional pain.

Despite the obstacles and the challenges that life presented, my heart was always tender towards God. This is the best wisdom that I can offer to any and to all. Being sensitive to the voice and the Spirit of God always put me in the right place with the right people at the right time. Like a Good Shepherd, God guided me to the Set-Go! Program for disadvantaged students as I was finishing up at the junior college. For some "strange" reason those posters caught my attention.

Mr. Silas Parnell, a black man on a mission, took one look at me as I entered his office to ask about Set-Go! and said, "I'm sending you to Fisk!" Mr. Parnell died a few years back, but not before sending hundreds of interested black students to colleges all across the nation. He specialized in finding colleges and universities with low black enrollment and taking van loads of Chicago students there for "free" education. One of his key challenges to students back in the day was, "Show me your library card." He taught that a library card was essential for a good education. He realized that it was for life and not for school that we were learning. I had a library card, and Mr. Parnell got me a full financial package to Fisk!

Being sensitive to the Holy Spirit, I talked to my mother; considering her continuing health decline, I decided that Fisk was too far away in case she needed me to get home immediately. Yet something within me wanted to, needed to, longed to be free, so even though I rejected the Fisk offer, Mr. Parnell helped me to get enrolled at Illinois State University, Bloomington-Normal, Illinois, only 135 miles away. I packed my few things, got on the bus, and went off to school.

When I arrived I discovered that I was short of funds. I went to a black woman in the financial aid office and was treated with disdain. She referred me to the head of the office, a white man. It just happened that he was a member of the white Assembly of God congregation that I attended while in college. He helped me to get a loan for that first semester so that I could remain in school. Then he became my "sponsor" to ensure my always having a work-study position for the rest of my time there.

I completed my BS in psychology and decided to go for a master's degree in education, which I completed in 1976. My whole family showed up for my first graduation, but Mama died before I completed my master's.

Early in June 1972 near the end of my third year at State, I had come home, on the bus. A couple of days later, my older sister, Esther, was going to be married and had asked our mother to be present at the courthouse for the ceremony. Our mother didn't feel good, wanted to conserve her energy for worship that night, so she asked me to go with my sister. After the ceremony, I went out with my sister and new brother-in-law for a meal to celebrate.

Upon returning home, I shared the details with my mother, who asked me to curl her hair as she prepared for church. My girlfriend and I decided to walk to church but we put my mother on the bus.

We waited for the bus to arrive, and I heard a commotion as the bus door opened. My mother was yelling and having difficulty catching her breath. My friend and I helped her into the narthex of the church. It was there, June 16, 1972, that my mother took her last breath. My sister went to Household Finance Company to pay for the burial. Then she and my brother came to our apartment and took every photo of our mother out of our home!

Because I'd worked as a resident assistant at college, I'd sent my mother an exquisite white lace dress for Mother's Day, and she was buried in it. This continues to be one precious memory of mine. We had her funeral at Faith Temple Church.

Basically, I was left all alone. Neither of my siblings was in a position to offer me a home and I would not have wanted to live with either of them. I was twenty, but very innocent and naïve. On the Sunday following my mother's funeral, Bishop Goldsberry raised an offering during worship that helped me decide to return to school.

I had a good friend, Shirley Sams, whose parents were Elder Solomon and Mother Ollie Sams. They were parents of nine children and they were the couple who told me to bring my few belongings and to move in with their family. Today, even though I no longer live in Chicago, I still consider it "home." The Sams and my father's widow, Viola Louise Chandler Allen, were the people who loved me and showed me all the favor that they had to offer. I treasure each of them for investing in me.

Although I was poor, abused, and left alone, God continued to open doors and to make ways for me, for I kept my heart tender towards God. I made it through college with only one loan! God's favor allowed me to be a resident assistant all through undergrad, and I had a graduate assistantship in graduate school. For all of my education, I have only had to repay one fifteen-hundred-dollar loan!

There were five job offers for me when I completed my master's degree. I accepted my first professional position at Coe College in Cedar Rapids, Iowa. Yes! There were black people in Cedar Rapids! I was hired to counsel black students and was made the diversity resident assistant, so that I had free housing. Black people lived in an area of town known as "the Section" and it was where I found and joined a Church of God in Christ where the pastor was Bishop Hurley Bassett. It was here that I discovered an album entitled "Everyman Wants to Be Free" by the Bethel Pentecostal Choir of Grand Rapids, Michigan. Mrs. Etterlene DeBarge, Bishop William Abney's sister and mother of the now famous DeBarge singers, sang lead on that title cut. That song found a resting place in my spirit and I determined that "one day" I was going to visit that congregation.

Two years later during a professional conference, I ran across an advertisement for the Advisory Center for Teens. Today it is called Arbor Circle. They were seeking a coordinator of Prevention and Education Services. Surely, I knew this field. I applied. I was hired. I moved to Grand Rapids and went immediately to Bethel Pentecostal Church!

I had a friend who lived in Grand Rapids, Diana Chandler, who was from Chicago. Diana worked at Pine Rest Social Services and belonged to First Assembly of God. She was able to assist me in so many ways, including finding my way to Bethel, for I wanted to be free!

Bethel Pentecostal is a member of the Pentecostal Assemblies of the World (PAW). I sat in the pews for a few months after introducing myself to Pastor Abney and telling him with insistence, "I want to join your church!" He met with me in his office one Tuesday night and listened to me share my heart desires and asked where I wanted to serve. I began to teach in the Sunday School Department. I joined the Nurses Guild. Then I became a part of a prayer group ministry, for I knew that I had a word of knowledge and wisdom to share. I was at peace, finding my freedom and desiring to assist others with finding theirs.

Elder Leon Dye was our Sunday school superintendent, whom I worked closely with wherever there was a need. I was a satisfied and happy camper, enjoying serving God where needed. One day in 1985, however, I stopped by the bishop's office about something minor. He sat and listened to me for awhile, then told me that Elder Dye had been talking to him about me. I sat, stunned and quiet. Finally, the bishop said, "Veneese, do you have something that you want to tell me?" Then I broke down and announced my call to ordained ministry.

Back then, seminary was not required. I was taken under close supervision by my pastor and taught personally, by both teaching and his role modeling. In November of 1995, I was ordained to Christian Ministry at the Bethel Pentecostal Church! I remain there, serving today. For many years, my primary focus was on the ministry to women. This was a special place for me, trying to help "my mother" and my sisters to find the freedom that Etterlene sang about so fiercely.

While serving God, both at my home church and in the community, other social service opportunities came my way. In 1981 a new federal program that emphasized adults returning to school was announced at Aquinas, a Catholic College in Grand Rapids. I became their director of Special Services for Continuing Education Students. I became like Mr. Silas Parnell, talking up, recruiting, and encouraging many adults that they could do the required work for their degrees. It was while doing this work of ministry that I was recruited to serve on the board of directors for Family Outreach Center.

Family Outreach Center was a young organization dedicated to offering mental health services to the inner city, urban community residents. With the help of a vital "community mother," Mrs. Ella Sims, people had been found, monies had been pulled together from a variety of sources, but the agency was on very shaky ground. I was appointed to the personnel committee following the layoff of the agency's first executive director.

The personnel committee sought to find the best individual to place in leadership. However, our task was to be honest and forthright about the state of the agency. No body was willing to take the risk. Finally, the committee turned to me and asked, "Veneese, why don't you become the executive director?" After *much* fasting and prayer, on September 7, 1983, I accepted the position and have been made both director and CEO.

It's the very best ministry that I have ever had.

Family Outreach Center serves people of color and those who are low income in Grand Rapids. We do all sorts of creative groups to help our people to be free! Family Outreach Center offers counseling; we do small groups; we go into jails and prisons; we hold after school programs; we have marriage and family groups; we do substance abuse treatment; we hold both victim and violator groups—and we do it all on a sliding scale that slides all the way down to free. I raise many offerings! Our budget today is well over three million dollars a year! And, despite all the opposition, government regulations, and restrictions, God keeps opening alternative doors and making ways for my "church members" and staff.

So far, I have not had the "right man" find me! As a single, saved clergywoman, I have many children through those I work with both at Bethel and at Family Outreach. I am persuaded that ministry is not limited to the confines of a building. My call is to be in ministry in the world and to serve those in the community. The challenges of my life have kept me sensitive to that small, still voice. Despite the many obstacles, stumbling blocks, and pain of my life, I have discovered a profound truth: God will lead us, like a good shepherd if we will trust, obey, and follow.

My prayer for you, my sister, is that the power of the Holy Spirit will fill you, lead you, guide you, and keep you as you allow the pain of your past to free both you and others as you minister in the days and years to come.

Sage Wisdom *on*
Pastoral Self-Care

Daisybelle Thomas-Quinney

Church of God

"The Spirit of the Lord is upon me, for I have been called to preach the Good News . . . !"

The details of the Tabernacle call up a visual feast that dazzles the imagination. The daily activities of art, design, and structural integrity called upon the highest skill of each person as the tent of meeting took shape: the cutting and setting of precious stones, the holy garments for Aaron and Moses; the embellished columns and the carved wood, the twisted yarns and tassels, the gold inlay, the ark of the covenant, the columns and the altars. The lavish beauty of each component creates an aesthetic picture of unrivaled heavenly glory, for beauty, worship, and practical use. . . . What might we gain for the church today if we elevated a wider range of the arts to an activity that honors the worship of God and shapes our interaction with society? Who might we win for the cause of Christ if we proclaimed the arts as a vocation useful to the church and a pathway to spiritual discovery? The desire to make art and surround ourselves with beauty and art has a holy origin and impetus that originates in the early pages of our sacred history. Our inheritance from the chosen people of Israel comes with the imperative to continue the legacy of art for heaven's sake and earth's harmony.

—Beverly J. Shamana, *Seeing in the Dark:*
A Vision of Creativity and Spirituality

I was a little Negro girl, born in the state of Alabama. I was born into a large family, with a father who was a farmer and preacher and a mother who cared for me and my many siblings. I was born into a struggling family where it was a challenge to be fed, clothed, loved sufficiently, supported adequately, and encouraged on a daily basis. But I was born into a religious family where the God of Abraham, Sarah, Isaac, and Rebecca were household topics.

DaisyBelle was my given name. Implied in this name is floral beauty and a nature that would attract others. But, families don't always use our given names, and my family nicknamed me Red. I was rough and she was tough. I would argue and Red would fight. I loved her family and I fought and sought love in return. But in this large family, my inner hunger was never satisfied. Yet, I have come to understand that even before I was born, the Spirit of God was upon me.

The Spirit of God brings favor. The Spirit of God brings a restlessness. The Spirit of God brings a searching, seeking, and inquisitive mind. And the Spirit of God sets those who are chosen for ordained ministry on a journey that will lead them into unknown directions. The Spirit of God is creative, it's imaginative, and it's far reaching. The Spirit of God is gentle, but firm. The Spirit of God is kind, but it's exacting and demanding of excellence. The Spirit of God is peaceful, but it's also frustrating to those who don't quite understand what's going on at the time.

Before my birth, the Beautiful Flower, Daisy Belle, was chosen, consecrated, and commandeered for the ministry of God. I recognized that I was different. But this reality of being different didn't bring with it a blessed assurance. My family simply thought that I was a difficult personality. But God always has a witness to the active presence of the Spirit.

An Alabama school principal took a kind liking to me. This woman of discernment began to spend time with this little feisty sister. She allowed me access to her home. And, greater yet, she allowed me access into her heart. For it really does take a village to raise a child. It is required of the whole Christian community to assist with the journey to a full anointing of the Spirit of God.

As I said, my journey to my anointing today began way before my birth. My anointing grew in my family home, as I walked in the farming footprints of my preaching father and listened to the faith of my praying mother. It was stirred, fanned, and cultivated in the public school system of one of the most segregated states in America. For DaisyBelle was God's beautiful flower. And God's daisies are hearty plants that annually are renewed and sustained on their journey.

"Famousity"—the challenge to become bold, bodacious, out of the box, transformed, different, and famous was spoken into my life and spirit by that old woman principal. That word, famousity, is a word that we all need to know. I want you to say the word with me. Famousity. For the fragrance of my life has touched you now, my sisters, and its attraction will help to pull you along the way. You cannot remain one of God's Beautiful Flowers without being changed. Famousity. Be on the alert for it!

A public school employee, a lowly paid principal in the segregated public schools in the rural area of Aliceville, Alabama, became God's prophet to me. She looked at me, who was filled with an anger that I could not explain, who stayed in trouble both at home and at school, fighting for what I thought were my rights, and this public servant declared to me, "Famousity is in you!"

What this older adult woman was trying to say to God's Beautiful Flower was, "The Spirit of God is upon you. You have been called to preach the good news of Jesus Christ to the poor in spirit. Red, you have been anointed by God, to heal the broken hearted you come in touch with along your journey. You have been sent to announce freedom, liberty, and a second chance to every captive to sin, and pardon to every prisoner sitting in places where they have confined themselves. God has chosen you, Beautiful Flower, to announce, to proclaim, and to teach that this is the year of God's amazing grace. Red, you have been chosen to tell the world that we can celebrate God's destruction of all of our enemies, and you are going to offer comforting words to everyone who grieves and who mourns. DaisyBelle, on your journey, you are going to care for the people of Zion. You are going to give them bouquets of daisies instead of the ashes that they expect. It is your responsibility to present messages of joy in sermons, in song, in drama, by your life, that contradict the world's messages of doom. Wherever you go, DaisyBelle, you will give people praising hearts in place of the brokenness that they will bring. Beautiful Flower, it is required of you to rename God's people Oaks of Righteousness. As you journey, tell them that they have been planted where they are by God to display God's glory and to rebuild for the honor of God."

When this prophet principle spoke the word "famousity" into my spirit, I didn't understand, couldn't comprehend, and had no idea what this adult was saying. Yet that word penetrated my very being and I began to walk differently, to expect more, to expand my horizons, and to set my sights on the far country.

The journey to an anointing takes God's servants to places where they will learn more to bring back. The journey to an anointing requires an enlarging of the heart so that all types of persons may be respected and loved. The journey to an anointing demands that there is study, learning, digging to be approved by the world as well as by the church. The journey to an anointing often sets us apart, makes us lonely, keeps us guessing and confused. For God is Mystery and nothing is ever easy, clear, or cheap. Beautiful flowers that bloom annually must have deep roots. They need much dirt thrown on them, and they are often cut back so that they will grow to their most full potential. It is not always fun being a Beautiful Flower for God. But it is required that you grow, remain steadfast, and keep on keeping on . . . because the Spirit of God is upon you.

My journey led me away from Aliceville to New York, where I went to work as a live-in au pair for a mob don and his family! It was there that I really did learn about the fine things in life as I made money to go to college. I completed college and went on to graduate school to receive a degree in psychology, so that I could deal with my own craziness! Then I taught elementary school for twenty-two years as I served my community in many different ways.

God gave me the creativity to establish a woman's theater group, and we made presentations at Friday night dinner groups. God gave me the Voices of Triumph and I begin to travel and present the history of Sojourner Truth, Harriet Tubman, and other powerful women in first-person voice. How I enjoy being a trumpet for Zion through this medium. Then God gave me Nelson Quinney, and my life took a real turn.

I'd given up all hope for marriage, for I'd passed the age of forty. I was an anchor in my family and a servant in my local community. But God knew that for the journey ahead, I would need backup. As I engaged in preclasses to prepare myself for seminary, I got a phone call from a former Sunday school student! He and his wife, Betty, had been my students when we all attended the Church of God in Lansing, Michigan. They had moved to Pennsylvania after his retirement. Then, Betty had been stricken with breast cancer and had died. After his period of grief, Nelson called me.

"Miss Daisy, can I come courting?" I was staying with a sister-friend, Rev. Dr. Eleanor Miller, in Evanston, Illinois, attending Garrett-Evangelical Theological Seminary when the phone call came. I almost passed out from fear! It took Eleanor to tell me, "Just say, 'Yes!'" I did, and he did, and we courted and got married in an awesome ceremony the next year in December. It was an anointed fantasy!

I moved to Pennsylvania and transferred to Pittsburgh Theological Seminary and commuted to complete my M.Div. degree. Nelson was my chief encourager, supporter, and maintainer of the home front as I prepared for full-time professional ministry. The day finally arrived that I was ordained by my denomination. I followed in the footsteps of my father! But, there was no church appointment, so I served as an unpaid associate at the local church of God. I began to gather women in that valley to begin another ministry. Oh, the ministry that we did together as I sought to follow the anointing of God on my life.

We lived in the valley for almost ten years and I went to work for a local university as an advisor to students, and then my ministry took another turn. I had given up thought of ever being a local pastor. I made myself content with the assignments God placed in my path. Life took a turn when my beloved spouse was relieved of his position as caretaker of our denomination's campgrounds and we had to move. We decided to return south. We chose to relocate to Montgomery, Alabama, where I'd be closer to my aging mom and Nelson would be closer to his family in Louisiana.

Immediately we went to the local Church of God, and the first thing that the pastor said to me was, "I've heard about you." I didn't know what that meant, but it didn't feel like a welcome mat was being put out for us! So we began to visit other denominations and felt like fish out of water. One day, that very same pastor called me and asked me to go and offer ministry to a little country church in Wetumpka, Alabama. There were about four families there. But, Nelson and I went. Eventually, I was installed as pastor. God had brought me full circle, back home.

Nelson has fully renovated that little church building, adding beautiful bathrooms, and we have a lovely fellowship hall where much ministry happens. I'm gathering children. I'm working with the local jail, conducting a choir there. I'm in fellowship with clergy-women of diverse denominations, and I'm adding personalities to my Voices of Triumph.

Our God is an awesome God! My journey has taken twists and turns that I never expected. My marriage and my pastoral assignment were never upfront plans for me, but God . . . ! The anointing of God has a life of its own. My prayer, my sister, is that one day you will see yourself as we see you . . . a Beautiful Flower, gifted, consecrated, committed, and qualified for the role of servant of the Most High God! To God is all the glory!

Linda H. Hollies

United Methodist Church

My grandmother did not subscribe to the *Lafayette County Democrat* newspaper, saying, "It's written by white folks, about white folks, for white folks." We received the *Chicago Defender* and the *Pittsburgh Courier* newspapers, although they were published in the far away northern cities and arrived by mail at least a week late.

Once a month, however, the *Democrat* published a women's page. The page held notices of weddings, engagements, and a few recipes that were sent in by readers with their names attached. Momma knew all the names and the maids who worked for them. On the morning when the women's page was published, as the maids passed the store on their way to work, Momma would choose one. "Sister Bishop, I hope you'll be able to bring me that page this evening." The woman would smile, proud to have been chosen. "Yes, ma'am, Sister Henderson. Be glad to."

The other women in the group would compliment the chosen one amid much laughter. That evening the maid would bring a folded newspaper page, and Momma would take a Babe Ruth from the icebox or a peanut patty from the candy counter. "You know I'm not trying to pay you. Just saying thank you."

Momma would sit down and gingerly put on her glasses. Immediately she would start tsking. (In the African American community, that gesture is called sucking your teeth.) I would wait for her comments. . . . We set together under the lamplight so many nights copying recipes that I can pull a perfect image of me and Momma bending over the kitchen table, scrutinizing the community news page.

—Maya Angelou, *Hallelujah! The Welcome Table*

Each one of us is a product of our environment, influenced by family, neighbors, education, race, and culture. As a child of the sixties, I loved the Temptations and "My Girl." There was something special to me about "The Tears of a Clown." And I enjoyed anything that Jackie Wilson sang, Red Foxx said, or Moms Mabley joked about. Yet, as a black Pentecostal, I also had a deep appreciation for Mahalia Jackson, Clara Ward, and the Caravans. I learned to dance the chicken, the funky chicken and the Chicago chicken. I knew how to do a big strong line as well as break down with the twist. For this was the music that I heard. This was the music and the people who influenced me while I was growing up. This is what my peers thought was popular. We are all products of our environments.

When I was growing up we were taught respect for our elders. We thought drugs were bought at a pharmacy. And we thought that you had to be married in order to have a baby! When I was coming up there was something called discipline. It was the art of making children behave. My parents had eight, of which I am the oldest, and when my Mom went grocery shopping, all of us had to go with her. We were a disciplined group, for Mama did not play! There was fasting and praying in our church. They called it spiritual discipline. They taught me that one had to learn how to live as a child of God. I was taught that giving up something that I liked as a personal sacrifice for what Jesus Christ had done for me was not a small matter. Every Tuesday and Friday were proclaimed fast days. We knew discipline. Being a member of God's church meant something to me then. And it means something significant to me now.

Something within me yet holds the reins. Something within me yet banishes the pain. There's something within me, called the Holy Spirit. And I want to share a bit of sage wisdom from my something within. The Scripture reading is from Paul's writing to a young man named Timothy, with whom Paul had a father-son relationship. Some years ago, in the city of Joliet, Illinois, a new friend, Harlene Harden, came to the very first United Methodist Church where I preached and said in her introduction to me: "God told me to pray for you!" That began a relationship that is dear to me today. My walk in ministry has now led her to several pastorates within the United Methodist denomination. So it's right, it's proper, and it's fitting that I say something meaningful to my daughters in ministry. And I could find no truer words to share than these: Remember Jesus Christ and preach God's Word!

People hear all types of news from the radio, television, and the print news media. They don't come to worship to rehearse bad news. People come to worship, seeking a Word from God. People come to worship seeking hope. People come to worship needing God's good news. They don't need your advice. They don't need your opinions. They don't even need to hear about your relevant experiences. Your call is to preach the Word of God. With an international opinion poll showing Jesus and George Bush vying neck to neck for the 122nd spot of fame, it's time that we teach the people of God about who Jesus Christ really is, for it's obvious that everybody does not know!

The church didn't begin in cathedrals, grand and gothic, but in house churches that began to grow, to spread, and to expand by the power of the Holy Spirit. As the little group of apostles began to do evangelism and Paul took the message of Jesus Christ to the gentiles, a fluid, loose organization began to change into a more highly structured institution. So, the Apostle Paul began to write his viewpoints, to provide explanations, and to establish doctrine and formal tradition that was to be followed by congregations in order to keep them in connection with Jesus Christ and this New Way.

The Pastorals demonstrate Paul's concerns with this newly emerging institution called the church of God. In them we deal with the protocol of worship, instructions for ministers, and practical consideration for administering to those who are needy in the congregation. However, among the chief concerns of the Pastorals is an emphasis on preserving the soundness of the faith.

Paul wanted them to remember Jesus Christ crucified, buried, and resurrected, for this is the foundation of our faith. Paul wanted them to remember and to rehearse the methods and the mannerisms that Jesus Christ had established. And, since Paul knew that we are all influenced by our environments, by our family, by our race, by our education, and by the culture around us, he called the church to establish boundaries. Paul called himself the "chief of sinners" before his experience of amazing grace. Paul did not have amnesia. Paul knew what he had done before his call by God. And Paul wanted the people of God, especially the ministers, the teachers, and the pastors to have a firm theology about Jesus Christ and his church. So, the Pastoral Epistles call out a warning to beware of heretical teachers and their influence among the people of God.

Too many Greeks had come into the church, bringing their songs about knowledge. Too many unchurched gentiles had come into the church bringing their songs of partying and casual sex. Too many different ways of thinking had danced into the church, causing confusion. This is what we call today synergism, or the mixing of many beliefs in order to keep the new "paying customers" happy! So Paul declared, "The devil is a liar!"

Jesus is the song of the church! Jesus Christ: him crucified, dead, buried, and sanctified is the praise of the church! Jesus Christ, our soon coming Sovereign, is the only tune to which we dance. Jesus Christ is the only reason for our ordination. And, Jesus Christ is the reason for the church.

Church members, visitors, and denominational officials will try to get you off track. Church members, visitors, and denominational officials will try to get you to dance to their tune. Church members, visitors, and denominational officials will make every attempt to persuade, influence, and browbeat you to win you over to their way of thinking. But always remember that there is only one note in the church of God. And that one note is the Word, the will and the way of God.

When church members, visitors, and denominational officials try to lead you astray, refer them to the Word. Stand on the Word. Meditate on the Word. Read the Word. Quote the Word. Pray the Word. Memorize the Word. Sing the Word. Ask every one who challenges you, "What biblical principle are you standing upon?" Always refer them back to the Word. For all scripture is inspired by God. All scripture is useful for teaching the people of God. All scripture is our source for refuting error, reproving lies, correcting the wayward, and guiding the feet of those who seek to live right. All scripture is essential for training the church in the discipline of righteous living. For the way of Jesus Christ is not popular in the church. The church wants a "happy meal theology" with a "let me have it my way" doctrine. But our call to ordination is one of standing for Jesus Christ and for calling people to him.

Paul ended up chained in prison and being executed for the sake of the gospel. Our call is a partaking in the suffering of Jesus Christ. For it was the church folks who betrayed and killed Jesus. The people did not all like Jesus, and they will not all like you either. They will enter your office with a smile on their faces and daggers in their hands. It's not because they are mean or out to get you. It's just because all of God's people are crazy! All of God's people have issues! And, like Paul, we are the chief of crazy people because we said, "Yes!" to God's call. We have to love God's people in the midst of the craziness.

We must preach Jesus Christ. We must teach that people are required to have a personal relationship with God that cleans up their lives. We have to preach that church people have been adopted into a new family, transformed by the renewing of our minds, and given the same song to sing that declares Jesus Christ as head of the church.

We must teach the people that we are all required to live morally clean, sexually pure, and holy lives before God in Christian community. We have to teach them that we are all baptized into the death of Jesus so that we can rise to new life in Jesus. And we must teach that our new life is more than about our receiving. Our new life teaches us how to be generous givers.

Teach the people of God with persistence. Teach them when they don't want to hear. Teach them. Convince them. Rebuke them. Encourage them. Love them. And do it with the understanding that your only job is to teach! The people must be receptive to hear and, then, to learn.

Sister Pastor, as you live, teach and preach Jesus Christ. Don't ever roll over and play dead before the people. Be bodacious. Be courageous. Endure the suffering that comes with doing the teaching of, touching of, and caring for souls. Carry out our call to ministry fully. Soon the trumpet will sound, time will fold into eternity, and Jesus Christ will appear. For faithfully living out your call, you will be able to hear God say, "Faithful servant, well done!" Until that time, just preach the Word!

(Preached October 2004 at Pastor Harlene Harden's installation in Chicago, Illinois.)

12 ᴄᴡ OH, WHAT NEEDLESS PAIN WE BEAR

Sharon Ellis Davis
United Church of Christ

Story-linking is a process whereby we connect parts of our everyday stories with the Christian faith story in the Bible and the lives of exemplars of the Christian faith outside the Bible. In this process, we link with Bible stories by using them as mirrors through which we reflect critically on the liberation we have already found or are still seeking. We also link with our Christian faith heritage by learning about exemplars who chose a way of living based on their understanding of liberation and vocation found in Scripture. By linking with Christian faith heritage stories, we may be encouraged and inspired by predecessors who have faced life circumstance with which we readily identify. The story-linking process can help us open ourselves to God's call to act in ways that are liberating for us and others and to decide how we will do this. It can also help us discern our vocation, formed and informed by the Christian story, as well as ways of accomplishing it. Story-linking is comprised of four primary phases: 1. engaging the everyday story, 2. engaging the Christian faith story in the Bible, 3. engaging Christian faith stories from the African American heritage, and 4. engaging in Christian ethical decision making.

—Anne Streaty Wimberly, *Soul Stories*

This chapter is the name of (what will one day be) a book I intend to write. You see, in this life we must all bear pain. No one is exempt from suffering pain. However, many of us bear needless pains. My story is one of needless pains that I hope no one else would ever have to experience. My story is also about triumph, victory, and being more than a conqueror. It is a story of how one person can take her miseries and turn them into ministry, mission, and a manifestation that "there is no secret, what God can do."

85

My name is Sharon Ellis Davis. I am a mother, a pastor, a professor, a policewoman, a chaplain, a wife, a grandmother, and a
survivor of domestic violence/abuse. Years ago when training to be
a police officer, I became involved with another police recruit. He
was quiet and I was quite social. He was not a good-looking guy or
what we would call "fine." In fact, he was not a good-looking
brother at all and, on top of that, he was a slow learner. This was
where I came into the picture. I thought I could help him with his
studies. So we began to meet nightly at my home for tutoring sessions. I was twenty-six years old. The young man whom I was then
dating was not pleased about these sessions in my home. My
boyfriend, however, was a married man, so I used these study
groups with the police recruit as an opportunity to make him jealous. Perhaps, I thought in a very naïve way, this would make my
boyfriend divorce his wife and marry me. Over time, the police recruit and I grew closer. He was very kind, considerate, and generous toward me with his gift giving. We both began our police ca-
reers in December 1978.

In January 1979 the city of Chicago had a major snowstorm that
debilitated the entire city. As police recruits, we were assigned to
work the midnight shift (11:00 at night until 7:00 in the morning),
shoveling snow from the various train station tracks and walkways.
On January 17, 1979, I had worked until 3:00 A.M. When I arrived
home I received a call from my boyfriend's cousin informing me
that my boyfriend had suddenly died of a massive stroke. He was
thirty-six years old. After being informed of his death, I believe I
had a nervous breakdown but was unaware of its occurrence. I was
devastated. My boyfriend was dead. I was alone with our three-
year-old daughter and did not know how to deal with his death.

When I called a female friend to express my pain, she told me
that I was lucky that God had only taken my boyfriend and not my
children. She admonished me for dating a married man (adultery,
she called it) and told me I ought to seek God's forgiveness. This
conversation led me through major cycles of feeling intensely guilty
over my choices and it paved the way toward my entering unhealthy
and abusive relationships. I had sinned before God. I was at risk of
God killing my children. Also, my life was in danger. And this was
all because of my choice to date a married man. As a consequence,
six months later, I married the police recruit.

In retrospect, I understand this marriage as my way of atoning for dating this married man and having his child. This marriage was my way of asking God's forgiveness and hoping to secure the lives of my children and myself. The pictures from my wedding told the story. My sister, who is manic depressive, was in her depressed state and she looked as if she was at the funeral of a very close relative. My children (ages three and seven), were standing next to me holding my dress crying hysterically during the time the minister (who was my father) said, "I now pronounce you husband and wife." My dad stood crying like he has done at all of our weddings or public performances. I was crying uncontrollably at the moment my father pronounced us husband and wife. While all of these things were occurring, the invited guests were clapping their hands in excitement, as they believed I was crying tears of joy.

In reality, however, I was having a nervous breakdown right before their very eyes. It was amazing no one knew what was going on but me. I knew I was grieving for my deceased boyfriend. I knew I did not love my current husband. I knew that I was making the wrong choice. Yet, I could not stop myself. This marriage became the marriage from hell.

After I said, "I do," all the niceness and generosity I had received in the past ceased. My new husband suddenly changed, and his actions toward me were emotionally as well as physically abusive.

He would seemingly have mood swings that could range from telling me he loved me to telling me he was going to tie me up to a car and drag me down the street. He put guns to my head and threatened to kill me. One time, he pulled the trigger but there were no bullets in the chamber of the gun. He had me arrested for crimes I did not commit, such as breaking his girlfriend's car windows out, setting fire to his (our) car, stealing drugs out of the crime laboratory (a place I was assigned to work), and sending a firebomb to my mother-in-law's house along with a threatening letter attached to it. I had my arms broken. I was driven to the lake, where he threatened to throw me in the water. I was given a venereal disease and then beat up as he accused me of giving him the disease. He isolated me from my children and threatened the lives of my parents. He stalked me by following me to church, to work, and to the home of my babysitter.

He harassed my friends and threatened my lawyer. He stole my car, then (with his police contacts) recovered it himself and kept it.

He stole my police uniforms, destroyed valuable family pictures. For two years he attempted to make my life a living hell. My abuser was never held accountable by the criminal justice system for his actions. As the victim, however, I experienced being arrested and finger-printed. I experienced being forced to take polygraph examinations, in which I failed. Incidentally, when he was finally requested to take a polygraph, he passed. Everything my abuser had done to me, he accused me of doing to him. And he got away with it.

Typical of domestic violence incidents, in between these abusive episodes, he would send me flowers and take me to nice places for dinner. One time, after the gun incident, he sent a singing telegram person to my job to sing words of apology and present me with an offering of balloons. All of these gestures were for the purpose of getting me to return home. And it worked. In the cycle of domestic violence, this is called the "honeymoon stage." You see, for every horrible thing my abuser did to me, I could name you five wonder-fully nice things he did for me in return.

In my fear and frustration, I cried for help from the police de-partment. I was convinced that the very institution I worked for could and would protect me. My cries, however, fell on death ears. No one heard my voice. No one took the abuse seriously. They (su-pervisors) would just admonish us to stop fighting (indicating that I was contributing to my own process of abuse). My abuser on one oc-casion dragged me out of our home while I was naked. He dragged me out of the house and threw me on the ground. He did this all while his police partner was in the police car waiting on him to come out of the house. The only words I heard his partner say were, "Come on, man." I went to my husband's commander in the district where he worked to express my fears for my life and to notify him of the abuse. I explained to the commander that I believed my abuser had some mental problems also. The explanation I received was they could do nothing about my claims because he was a good police officer and made plenty of arrests. Therefore, there was noth-ing in his police work that indicated there might be a problem.

Still trusting the criminal justice system to protect me, I visited my attorney, who was a retired Chicago police lieutenant. I filed for divorce and asked for some type of protection. The courts gave me the marital home. My husband, however, consistently harassed me in the house and I had to leave. He moved into the house and moved all of our furniture out of the house. The judge gave me the rights to recover from the house all that was mine, but when I arrived at the house, everything was gone. He, in front of the judge, accused me of stealing the furniture. I ended up paying for the furniture I never received. The courts could not take action because nothing could be proved. Still trusting the system, I volunteered to take a polygraph test, which I believed would show the department that I was right and my abuser was the guilty party.

I paid more than five hundred dollars to take the test. The test results proved that I was the guilty party. I was devastated again.

Later, after the accusations continued to surface, the department insisted that I take an official polygraph test along with my abuser. Out of fear that I would fail the test again, I refused. My attorney, however, convinced me to take the test. He declared my innocence and he had faith in the process. We both took the test. He passed. My results were inclusive. I soon learned that I could not trust or depend on the criminal justice system for protection. Where, then, could I go for safety? Where could I go to get permission to walk away from something that was killing me psychologically, spiritually, and possibly even physically. Where could I turn for my voice to be heard? This answer was obvious, the church.

Before I could even get to the church for help, however, I was hearing voices inside of me from the churches in my past. These voices were not voices of liberation. These voices were those of guilt, shame, blame, condemnation, and damnation. These voices kept me in my guilty state, unable to have any agency that would give me permission to leave my abusive relationship. All I could access was the God who was this boogie man in the sky who was ready, willing, and able to punish me for all the wrong I had done. And my sins were many. Right on the top of the list of sins was adultery. I thought, God must have been punishing me for dating this married man. This abuse was my fault. I should have known my sins would catch up with me. These patterns of guilt, shame, and blame were planted in my head long before I was every abused. They had been there since childhood.

As a child, I knew I had my place as a woman. Women were not leaders. Women, as I saw them, wore the little white hats and brought water and juice to the pastor before and after he preached. Women were the cooks and the caretakers of the church (especially for the pastor). Male pastors got invited to dinner after church and got to eat good fried chicken. Male pastors got their own parking spots and their clothes taken to the cleaners by the women of the church. In the meantime, women got to serve the pastor. As a child, I knew well my place. I grew up knowing the place of women. Women were to be silent and serve men.

There was no voice inside my own head that ever gave me permission to leave an abusive relationship. There was no voice inside my head that told me I had value and was deserving of love, care, and affection. The only voices I could access were the voices that placed on me blame, shame, guilt, and condemnation. Even today those voices that seek to oppress women continue to exist in the church. Consequently, like me, too many women suffer much needless pain. This is not simply the pain of domestic violence. I am referring to the pain of misinformation, disempowerment, disenfranchisement, devaluing, and other forms of oppressions placed upon women that allow and open the doors toward their entering into unhealthy relationships and enduring even more pain and suffering. These pains are needless and can be avoided if men and women of the gospel would stand up and tell the truth.

After experiencing such disappointments and betrayals, I have often been asked how I remained in the police department and the church, especially as a minister and pastor. First of all my answer is simple. I believe in these institutions (police and church) and their potential. I believe both institutions are necessary and vital as institutions of justice, accountability, truth, protection, and, especially for the church, liberation. I could not think of two better places toward which to commit my time and efforts. My presence within these institutions, however, includes and depends upon my ability and divine mandate to hold them both accountable for who they are called to be.

Where the church is concerned, I learned that the failure was not with God, it was with human interpretation. I can and will critique the criminal justice system and the church because of and out of my love for both institutions. The black church especially has historically been the place where voices rang out to fight racism. My voice is now added to those who will speak out against sexism, racism, gender oppression, homophobia, and other oppressions that cause anyone to feel as though they are less than they are in the eyes of God. If God does not care about the color of our skin, then certainly God does not care about whether we are male or female as a delineation of who can serve as pastors or in leadership in the church. To make these wrong judgments and assertions is to cause people to suffer needless pain. And God knows that we already have enough pain in our lives.

I speak to leaders in the church, and especially to the black church. If we are ever going to break the code of silence in the criminal justice system as well as in the church, we are going to have to take a long hard look at ourselves, our actions, our attitudes as well as the ways we teach, preach, and practice our theology. People come to the church long before they go to a shelter. How we minister with them could literally cost them their life! The words of Michael Jackson's "Man in the Mirror" are profound. If we want to change something, the change must come from within us.

The Bible says that we should not look for the speck in someone else's eyes while there is a log in our own. Leaders in the church, especially those entering pastoral ministry, need to spend a great deal of time discovering who they are and what biases (theological, doctrinal, and relational) they bring along with them that may injure God's people. In a time where people need to run to the church, many are running from the church out of fear and revictimization by the very same institution that claims to be a "shelter in the times of storm."

How did I respond to the injustices I faced as a child and an adult? First by taking responsibility for the wrong I had done and asking God's forgiveness. Second, I committed myself to a spiritual growth and a counseling program that enabled me, while studying for ministry, to rid myself of the leftovers of negative self images and the resulting behaviors toward myself and others.

I finally found the courage, strength, and permission within myself to leave my abusive marriage. But the healing process seems like it takes an eternity, for as the song says, "there's always something there to remind you . . ." Healing deep wounds takes work and dedication. This work can take years but it is worth it.

Third, I committed to teaching and preaching a gospel wherein people will know that they are loved and accepted by God for who they are and not what others believe they *should* be. I believe this is a difficult task for many ministers who believe they are the holders and keepers of "the truth." They will dispense this truth until it hurts others, in the name of God. Please know that when you engage in this behavior you re-injure and re-traumatize people who are already injured.

Finally, I took the struggle one step further. I decided to do something about the injustices. In the police department I was instrumental in forming an advisory committee that addressed and brought attention to domestic violence in police homes. This committee was responsible for the department hiring its first civilian advocate to work exclusively with the wives of police officers who were being abused. I continue to this day serving on boards that are committed to work against domestic violence (including the Chicago Abused Women's Coalition, the Mayor's Office on Domestic Violence, and others). As part of my Doctor of Ministry program (1995), I began a church-based domestic violence ministry in my home church of more than five thousand members. I speak professionally and nationally on issues of domestic violence, pastoral care, and the church, especially as it intersects with race, class, gender, and the criminal justice system.

I speak, prophetically, to power. I teach a course called Sexual and Domestic Violence to seminarians. Recently I graduated with my PhD. My dissertation is titled "Hear Our Cries: Breaking the Gender Entrapment of African American Battered Women." In this program I was able to heal even more through writing. It also took my advocacy to another level, that of academic activism. Bearing "needless pain" is difficult. This is why clergy must see and take their role as healers seriously. We must use every voice and gift that we have to bring God's reign closer and closer. We must minister in ways that will allow people to experience a little bit of heaven right here on earth.

A sister clergyperson and I began a new church several years ago with help from the United Church of Christ. We are located in an impoverished area, and it is not a place where people rush to pastor. It is not attractive and certainly we are not there for the money. There is none! I serve as senior pastor, she serves as my associate, and my current husband, a police officer who holds master's degrees in both divinity and business administration, is the administrative pastor. Recently we hired a youth pastor to join the staff.

Many people have asked me why, with a Master's of Divinity degree, a Doctor of Ministry degree, and now a Doctor of Philosophy degree, I am out there when I could have my choice of churches to pastor. Many people have looked down on our ministry in this very impoverished, gang and drug infested area. I really don't have a particular answer for them. In fact, sometimes I feel the same way. All I really know is that God has brought me from a mighty long way. I know that many people are hurt and wounded and many of their wounds have come from the church. Wherever God calls me, I want to give the message that they are loved and that they have worth. Wherever God calls me, I want to be in places where we can give the message of healing, hope, and wholeness.

Our church is named "God Can Ministries." This name came to me on a night when I had, once again, almost given up on attending church. I had decided, enough with church. I'll just visit and serve God, but not pastor. I heard these words: "When you can't move this mountain that is standing in your way, I got an answer for you, God can! When you can't find the strength to face another day, God can! God can do more than you could ever ask or think. God holds us in God's mighty hands. When you can't find your way, just remember this, I say, God can!" Thus, I finally knew the name of the church I would pastor as well as my life's mission. As long as God gives me strength I will do my part to ensure that the church is a place were all voices can be heard, all people will be welcomed, and all people can hear the message of salvation and liberation.

13 ∾ THE DIVINE DESIGN
Be an Original Clergy Woman

Linda H. Hollies
United Methodist Church

It is important to recognize that, in our work for justice and reconciliation, we often do not have control over the results. If our identity and our worth are wrapped up in our work and our success, we will rise and fall emotionally and spiritually and be ineffective in the battle. The practice of Sabbath reminds us that our worth is wrapped up in God. It brings us back home to the fact that our service is an act of worship—a responsive act of love to the One who gave his life for us. The Sabbath is possibly the most fundamental Christian discipline, because it goes to the heart of our understanding of salvation. We are saved, given worth and identity, and promised a bright destiny by grace. We do not earn it. It is a gift. Sabbath uniquely leads us into experiencing the core of our conviction that we are saved by grace through faith and that it is not of our doing—so we rest.

—Brenda Salter McNeil and Rick Richardson,
The Heart of Racial Justice

Once upon a time, I was invited by my clergy brother, Rev. Dr. Michael Carson, to sit in on a denominational gathering for those who were seeking ordination. The men came in "sharp" and the women came in wearing the obligatory black and white suits and blouses. But there was one sista whose outfit was off the hook in its design and presentation. She was beautifully made up with a hairstyle to beat the band. Beside her, the other women looked dowdy!

When my brother asked me to address the group as an outside consultant, I had the outstanding woman stand, and I spoke to her

originality in "following the rules." Prayerfully, she made a difference to the other women in her class, for she showed them how to be
distinct and original as they stand before the people of God. I realize
that the argument has been made that what we wear can distract
people. And I argue on the other side that when we don't present
ourselves with distinction, we will distract people just as well.

The Ultimate One has been very careful and very deliberate about
what we are to wear, how we are to dress, and who we are to represent. Our God did not leave what we are to wear to the priest or the
prophet. There was no planning team, design committee, or consultation group called when our wardrobe was fashioned. The Beginner of
Beginnings fashioned for us with specificity and originality. Nothing
was left up to chance, for the Divine Designer had us in mind.

The original design was formally introduced in Egypt when
God instructed the Hebrew slaves, on their way to freedom, to go
and ask of our ancestors their finest clothing, and jewelry of silver
and gold. After these former slaves reach the wilderness, God asked
them to participate in the construction of the tabernacle. The instructions are very specific! Exodus 25:1–9 reveals that God demanded gold, silver, bronze, blue, purple, and scarlet stuff and fine
twined linen. The reason? "Let them make me a sanctuary that I
may dwell in their midst. . . ."

The Omnipotent One, the Awesome One, the Majestic One was
coming to live among formerly homeless slaves! This God wanted
to come, willed to come, and longed to come. But the dwelling place
had to be right! The earthly inhabitation of the Creator had to have
some semblance of that eternal home. The only buildings ever con-
structed that were perfect from the very beginning and never
needed any further refinement or alteration were the ark of Noah,
the tabernacle, and the Temple of Solomon. Each one was designed
by divine revelation. Each one was just a symbol of the earthly presence of Almighty God.

The design of all of the intricate specifications of the tabernacle
were specified by God, committed unto Moses, and built by those
chosen, called, and consecrated. Every detail had a prophetic significance that reflected our perfect salvation, through Jesus Christ. The
Chief Architect filled the tabernacle with breath-taking splendor,
exquisite glory, and magnificent beauty that simply reflected the
character and personality of the Most High God.

Afterwards, the Chief Architect began to design for those who were to minister in this great house. "They [the skilled workers] shall make these . . . sacred garments: . . . they shall receive and use gold, blue, purple, and scarlet stuff, and . . . fine twined linen, skillfully woven and worked" (Exod. 28:4–6 AMP) God named for Moses the craftspeople who would make these holy garments. The reason is in verse two: "these garments shall be for honor [some versions say glory] and for beauty."

The workmanship had to be superb. The skill level required was excellence. The reasons are stated in Exodus 28:43: "this shall be a perpetual [an everlasting, binding, and eternal] statute" for priests who represent God. God has a love of excellence. God has a flair for the dramatic. God has a penchant for the exotic and the flamboyant. For God is glorious, more than splendid and mighty in majesty. There is little in the design of the tabernacle or the clothes of the priesthood that was drab, dull, or boring. God demanded the most vivid colors, the most brilliant hues and the most extraordinary shades. There was nothing allowed to appear as shoddy, second class, or inferior "stuff." God demanded the very best and the most precious articles to be found. Every piece represented the place where the Shekinah Glory of the Living God dwelled.

God designed it. God orchestrated it. God created it to represent God's own awesome self. So what we wear is not a simple indication of who we are, it's a profound statement about who God is! What we wear is a sign of our call, our authority as priest, and our position as women, called to reflect God. We sing, "Lord, prepare me to be a sanctuary," but we don't dress like God's sanctuary! Sisters, we are the temples of God. We are the spokespersons for God. We are the royal priesthood, the called out ones, the holy nation. And, we ought to always look like it. Too many of us are walking around trying to look the way others have told us we ought to look. Too many of us are not sure why we wear it, but since "the big boys" wear it, we want to wear it too. But, always remember, when Sister Eve stepped out in her newly fashioned fig leaf, which God did not design, that little piece of human-made apparel was not blessed, sanctified to her use, or left to dry up and die on her! God snatched it off and whipped up a Designer original!

Girlfriends, we serve an awesome God. And to be like God means you have to be daring, adventuresome, colorful, extravagant, bold, bodacious, courageous, and beautiful. It requires guts, grit, and gumption to defy the world and to hang with the Designer's way out, striking, and nontraditional garb. For it's flashy. It's attention getting. It was designed by God to show the perpetual beauty and the glory of the One who called us to wear it! Does what you wear reflect God's glory, brilliance, and splendor? Far too many of us have heeded the voices of those who say, "Don't draw attention to yourself." But, that's not the Divine Designer's way! We have been called to "twinkle, twinkle, little star"!

Wearing dull, solemn colors, looking dowdy and depressing, is ungodly. The divine designs we are to wear demand presence. For we have been given the sacred duty to be a called out as witnesses, ambassadors for God, and revealers of the mysteries of the ages. The clothing is not to tell folks to see you and me. But, what we wear is to pull the mind of the people toward the One we stand for! Psalm 45:9 (AMP) declares, "The Kings' daughter are among your honorable women; at your right hand stands the queen in gold of Ophir." Our wardrobe, from underwear out, is a symbol of the perfect humanity of Jesus Christ. Our clothing is to symbolize our spotless, but beautiful life; our pure, but visioning mind; our clean but generous heart; and our constant and unfailing purpose to let the world see Jesus in our life!

As you look at the New City of Heaven in Revelation 21 you find a city shimmering in a pulsing light, with walls of jasper, streets of pure gold, translucent as glass. The foundations are garnished with every precious gem imaginable and the gates are of pearl. This is where the Eternal One lives! This is where we are journeying to be forevermore. God wants us to start now, dressing for the homecoming. It's time to get your wardrobe right! Put on the divine design!

This chapter was excerpted from a teaching session Rev. Dr. Linda H. Hollies conducted at the Holy Convocation for African, African-American, and Caribbean Clergy Sisters held in August 1997 in Atlanta, Georgia.

Sage Wisdom *on*

Community Ministry

Patricia Spearman

United Methodist Church

Women still suffered under patriarchal notions about the place of women. Many women are unnamed . . . the major difference in Christian Scriptures is the way Jesus interacted with women. Jesus defied patriarchal custom and treated women with respect and honor. He counted among his disciples and friends women of substance. Although the general plight of women was not changed, their connection with Jesus made a difference in how they saw the world and opportunities available to them.

The gospel writers included women in Jesus' genealogy, and women played a major role in the ministry and work of Jesus. He did not exclude women, and he regarded them as equals to men. The first Christian evangelists and preachers were women who testified about how things had changed because of Jesus of Nazareth. When the male disciples fled after Jesus' crucifixion, the women remained. When the male disciples were hiding in the Upper Room after Jesus' burial, the women were at the tomb. When Jesus appeared after the resurrection, the women were there. Jesus commanded the women to go and tell men—women were the first preachers!

Jesus ushered in a new way of relating to women, but the larger society continued its patriarchal ways.

—Barbara J. Essex, *Bad Girls of the Bible:*
Exploring Women of Questionable Virtue

Seminary teaches a future pastor how to cope with traditional challenges in the parish community. In many cases, it is not equipped to teach realm building principles, such as community outreach, networking skills, or involving the congregation in community transformation. I believe that, after the singing, testifying, shouting, and preaching, we have an imperative mission as followers of Christ. We must go into the world and *re-present* God. We have to re-present God to those who are lost, left out, kicked to the curb, and can't relate to the one dimensional message of the "traditional church." For many church folk, the mission of winning souls to Christ begins and ends with this statement—"Come to my church and be saved." That's' what I call trying to represent God. We re-present God through an intentional and sustained commitment to the practical application of God's Word.

Jackson Chapel UMC is in an ethnically and economically diverse area of San Marcos, Texas. There are joys and challenges associated with an assignment to this particular community. I asked God for wisdom and a sense of urgency in order to develop a prophetic ministry for the church and the community at large. As a church, we prayed for God to show us how to reach those in the immediate community.

Some people suggested a food pantry, but several organizations in town provided that service. Someone else suggested a clothes closet for needy families. The idea sounded great—but the devil was in the details. I asked the person recommending that as an outreach ministry about staffing, sorting, and storage space for the clothes, and about how they would determine client eligibility. The idea fizzled.

I did not see that as failure. I believe that is a healthy way for faith communities to discern how God is calling them to fellowship with those living in close proximity of the church. All too often, people see a successful outreach program done by another church and they want to co-op the program. The results give communities fifty food pantries or clothes closets for the needy while ignoring the needs of children and seasoned citizens within the community. A prayerful and deliberate search will help pastor and people discern how God wants to be re-presented through the tangible ministry of faith communities. The answer comes in ordinary situations, but your work will bring extraordinary results.

One Sunday I noticed many of the children in the elementary Sunday school class had a difficult time reading and comprehending the material. As we worked to help our children with their materials, it dawned on me that the problem might transcend our church. Our community had an exceptionally high dropout rate among the poor, minority, and special circumstance citizens (teen mothers/ fathers, children of immigrants). That was an epiphany. The epiphany birthed our first outreach ministry—Rearing Our Own to Succeed (R.O.O.T.S.)

God had a plan for our church to reach people in the neighborhood—this was a clarion call to action. We made this a prayer priority. Whatever you decide to do in terms of ministry and community outreach, you have to undergird with prayer. Prayer reinforces the difference between "realm building" and "church membership building." After the prayer warriors prayed, the ministry team began to develop a strategic plan to reduce the school dropout rate and increase the number of students entering post secondary institutions. There are several areas of planning and consideration necessary for a successful outreach ministry. I'll use our R.O.O.T.S. program to illustrate the chronology.

GET YOUR CHURCH ADMINISTRATIVE BODY ON BOARD

I brought the idea to the next administrative board meeting. The motion passed unanimously and we had eight people to volunteer their service to ensure success. We divided the project into phases and asked the church membership to commit to at least one phase.

DEVELOP A WORK PLAN WITH INTERMEDIATE MILESTONES

The high dropout rate among minorities and low-income students was detrimental to *all* members of our community. Our plan included (1) talking to parents and other significant adults involved in the children's life, (2) developing ways to fund the program, (3) contacting educational professionals and other subject matter experts (SMEs) and enlisting their support, (4) developing the program metrics to evaluate the program, and (5) recruiting children for the program and establishing a clear reward system.

ESTABLISH A NETWORK SYSTEM AND USE IT

I was heavily involved in the local community and used my contacts with local government and business leaders to build partnerships for the project. Establishing a network system with business, government, and other community leaders is a critical aspect of development and outreach. I always find it helpful to visit and introduce myself to community leaders and business entrepreneurs during within the first month of my assignment to a new church. I ask about their business, goals, and length of time in their particular field, and I ask them to begin thinking of ways that our church can collaborate with them to improve/strengthen our community.

IDENTIFY YOUR PERSONAL AND CORPORATE PASSIONS AND FIND PARTNERS FOR THE PROGRAM

Your passion will give you the "fire in the belly" to keep on keeping on during the challenges of the development stage. My passion has always been education—learning and teaching. Once you have identified your passion, find people of like minds and complementary strengths. You may find some in your congregation, but do not limit your search to "church folk." In fact, you will expand your ministry reach if you look for cohorts among people in secular businesses.

SELECT A LEADER FROM THAT GROUP AND DEVELOP A FINANCIAL PLAN OF ACTION

Once you identify members of your congregation who are willing to work with you in this endeavor—to carry the project forward—it is important for the group to feel ownership in the emerging outreach ministry as soon as possible. The book of James states it exactly right, "Faith without works is dead." You will need consistent financial support in order to ensure long-term success. Most churches do not have unlimited finances. Don't worry; you can still get the job done if you're willing to be creative and tap into some of the many unconventional sources.

While working to develop our tutorial program, I asked members of my sorority at the local university to consider the program as a potential community project. They selected our program and provided at least ten volunteers per week. That gave us people to help the children with reading and other homework assignments. I asked one of the seasoned citizens organizations to help recruit surrogate grandparents to read to preschool children.

The summer between the second and third year of the program, I made an appeal to the local teachers' organization asking for assistance with program expansion and curriculum development for a SAT/ACT study program. They agreed to help us for two school years. The combined gifts of in-kind contributions totaled more than three thousand dollars per year. We didn't have all the finances in the church budget, but working with like-minded people helped to bridge the gap between the amount on hand and the amount needed to sustain the programs.

We didn't have a great surplus of money, people, and talent, so I improvised. I had several friends working with Austin Independent School District, Huston-Tillotson College, and the University of Texas who agreed to assist in this endeavor. Chris Cain, a licensed practicing counselor (LPC), drove sixty miles twice a week to provide individual and family counseling services for the participants.

SURROUND YOURSELF WITH EXCEPTIONALLY TALENTED PEOPLE

I'm a visionary. I can see possibilities and develop "broad plans" for a program. Getting the details arranged during implementation is not my gift. Sisters, don't be afraid to surround yourself with ministry partners who have strengths in your areas of challenge. Felicia Hopkins had recently answered her call to ministry and was completing her first year of seminary. Felicia has a strong background in corporate management—dealing with operational details. I gave her the assignment to track student progress and collate the data.

IDENTIFY A BENCHMARK, EVALUATION METRICS, AND REWARDS PROGRAM

You have to have a benchmark and metrics in order to quantify the progress of your programs. With parental approval, we were able to use the results of the Texas Assessment of Academic Skills (TAAS) Test, teacher's testimonies and success stories of our students to complement the raw data. Felicia used the results to develop an "Appeal Presentation" to businesses. During the fourth year of the program she was able to get several stores in the mall signed on as partners in the program. They donated gift certificates for movie tickets, ice cream, hamburgers, and name-brand athletic shoes/jerseys. Every student in the program received some type of reward at the end of each grading period. This helped to reinforce our message of student success.

The R.O.O.T.S. program was operational five years. During that time, we saw a decrease in the student drop-out rate (physically and mentally) and an increase in college applications. The superintendent of schools presented our church with the Superintendent's Outstanding Award for Service to Students. In his speech, he sited the R.O.O.T.S. program as a significant and positive factor in the dramatic turnaround.

I've moved on to other areas of pastoral ministry as I reflectively write about my experience at Jackson Chapel. It was here that I was cited by the United Methodist Church with the Evangelism Award and featured in *Jet* magazine for my ministry with this group of inspired laity. The fire in my belly for both learning and teaching simply overflowed onto them. They caught my vision and we worked together. I know that this method works and I, as a sister, offer it to you.

15 ∾ I Have a Story to Tell You

Paulette Sankofa

African Methodist Episcopal Church

Be not dismayed what ere betide, God will take care of you. / Beneath God's wings of love abide, God will take care of you.

—Civilla D. Martin, "God Will Take Care of You"

To keep your queenly connection with the ultimate power source you have to stay prayed up. Prayer is the best vehicle for connecting with God. Pray with honesty. If you feel good today, pray and say, 'God, I feel good today.' If you feel lousy, say so too in prayer. God already knows what you are thinking, so you are not fooling anybody. Pray a long prayer or make it a short prayer. You could even pray this inclusive Prayer of Jesus: "God in heaven, hallowed be your name; your [realm] come, your will be done, on earth as in heaven. Give us today our daily bread. Forgive us our sins as we forgive those who sin against us. Save us from the time of trial and deliver us from evil. For the [realm], the power, and the glory are yours now and forever. Amen."

Prayer gives you the ultimate source of confidentiality. There are some secrets that should only be trusted with the one who will never tell. . . . Meditation is an excellent means of connecting with God. Meditation means that you focus your mind on the goodness of God and how awesome God is. Meditation is helpful because sometimes we expend mental energy on unproductive things. It has been said that we often "major in the minors." Those thoughts that center on anger, pain and rejection can paralyze you. Meditation is all about how God can liberate you and your thoughts. Please do not confuse this with Eastern religions. Christians can and should meditate. Even the psalmist wrote in Psalm 27:4 that he longed to spend time meditating: "One thing I have asked of God, that I will seek after; to live in God's house all the days of my life, to behold the beauty of God and to inquire in God's temple."

—Sheron C. Patterson, *Put on Your Crown:*
The Black Woman's Guide to Living Single . . . and Christian

I always introduce myself in the same way. My name is Paulette
Eloise Handley Sankofa. I was named after my maternal grand-
mother, Pauline. Eloise was the name given to me by my eldest aunt,
Elizabeth, who was so very affectionately known as "Aunt Lizzie."
The name Handley is the name worn by my father. The name
Sankofa is the name I have given myself. Sankofa is from the Akan
vernacular of the people of Ghana, West Africa, meaning that as we
move forward, we must always reach back to embrace what we have
left behind and bring it forward with us and learn from that past.
The symbol of Sankofa is that of a mythical bird that flies forward
while reaching back for a precious egg that it carries. For me,
Sankofa is also a symbol of community; of history, present and future; of seeking knowledge and embracing wisdom. I wanted my
name to be an educational tool along my continued journey as edu-
cator, student, and woman of faith and wisdom.

I am the firstborn child of Luella and Walter Handley and the
elder sister of Walter Michael Handley. I am the aunt of Alexandra
and Lauren Handley. I am a child of the sixties, a baby boomer, and
a womanist thinker who has survived and even thrived, against all
odds, as an African American woman growing up in the racist, sex-
ist U.S. culture. But above all of that, I am a woman called by God
to serve God's people.

I was raised in St. Louis, Missouri, where I was a member of
Scruggs Memorial Christian Methodist Episcopal Church most of
my life. I have so many power-filled memories of that church and its
congregation. I can still vividly remember Miss Janie Smith, one of
the elder women of the congregation. On most Sunday mornings, at
some point, she would leap to her feet and start to run all around the
sanctuary and praise God. I was a little girl then, but I can remember thinking to myself that I wanted to know what she knew and
feel what she was feeling. I can remember Rev. Cunningham's
preaching. My mother often tells the story of how I would stand up
on the pew and shout out "Preach, Ham, preach!" I couldn't have
been more than five years old.

Growing up I saw pastors come, and I saw pastors go, but there
was never a woman as the senior pastor. I don't know if I really
thought about it one way or the other at the time. When I accepted
my call, there were still few women in ordained ministry in my denomination. However, at Scruggs, I was fortunate to have my elder

cousin, Rev. Eutophia Hudspeth, as a role model. She had been ordained a few years before and served as an assistant to the senior pastor. She's quite a marvelous and devoted woman. I have watched her continue to serve despite sharp criticism from friends, strangers, and even loved ones. She continues to be a source of spiritual support and wisdom for me.

In retrospect, I know that I began my journey in ministry many years before I accepted my call on that faith-filled date of December 28, 1991. My call to ministry actually began in my mother's womb. One afternoon, my mother came to my office at Christ Community United Methodist Church, where I was the pastor, and she sat down and told me the story. It was much like the story of the biblical Hannah, mother of Samuel. She told me about the fact that she had lost other children before I was born and that she had prayed to God for a child. With tears in her eyes, she talked about the promise she had made to God, that if she could just be given a child, she would return that child back to God. She said that in me her prayers had been answered.

In 1991, I accepted my call to ministry. I thought right away that I should tell my pastor. After all, he had always been so nice. I expected him to be as excited as I was, but he told me that he wanted me to think about it for five years. He explained that he wasn't sure that God had called me, and he wanted me to be sure. He gave me a few texts to read and that was about it. My response was to tell him about my life and how God had been there all of the time beckoning and calling me. I told him about my first "close encounter" with God, when I had been married and my former husband tried to strangle me to death, and how God had saved my life and how that voice, which only God has, had spoken to me and told me that I was going to be a minister.

That was back in 1971. I went on to tell him about how one day in 1982, while traveling down a highway in Atlanta, Georgia, the Holy Spirit had come over me and I pulled over on the highway and began to praise God, as that same voice came back to me and told me that I was chosen by God. None of this seemed to make sense to help this fella. He couldn't understand why I had no doubt that I was called by God to serve in ordained ministry. If this guy only knew of all of my efforts to get away from, avoid, and just down right ignore my call he would have been astonished—but God just kept right on calling. I finally told him about how on December 28, 1991, God had once again come to get my attention. It was much akin to what Paul had experienced on the road to Damascus. I told him about how the Spirit of God had touched me from the top of my head to the bottom of my feet, and how I found myself prostrate on the floor praising God, and how God's voice once again had spoke to me, only this time it said, "Clean up your life; I've got work for you to do." Sometimes on our journey in ministry, things can seem really strange, or not even make sense. But God's vision is so far beyond what we're able to comprehend, that we just have to have faith. I promised God that I would go anywhere and do whatever God called me to do, and that's the path I've followed every since.

Despite sharing all of that with my pastor, he just basically said "I can't relate to what you're saying," and continued to set me aside. I decided to leave my home church. That was my first step-out on faith. I went to another denomination. My first experience there was to be treated inappropriately by an African American male colleague, who was also supervising me in the ordination process. Things got so bad that I reported him to a member of the Ordained Ministry Team and to the bishop. I must admit, she took action and called us in for a meeting. Of course Rev. "Inappropriate" denied everything and said some very uncomplimentary things about me. But, thanks be to God, I did have tapes of his inappropriate messages. I was finally forced to change my membership to another congregation in order to continue, and I was able to become a student pastor. However, I was penalized for the year that Rev. "Inappropriate" would not certify. Yet, I had to stand up to this guy. I thought about the women who would come after me, and what this might mean in their journey.

I stayed with that denomination for ten years. For four of those years, my mentor was the same pastor who came to my assistance, Rev. Bill Richardson. He was the pastor of the church where I served as student pastor. He was the most unlikely of mentors for me, a middle-aged, city-raised, African American woman. He was a white man from rural, southern Missouri. But he was also an old civil rights worker who had faced his share of conflict because of his preaching and living out of his social gospel principles. Rev. Richardson and his wife, Ann, were two of the greatest blessings I ever received in my life. They helped me to heal from the trauma I had faced and always encouraged me to stay focused on God's call and the powerful heritage of the African American congregation where I had grown up. But he also cautioned me that sexism wasn't the only challenge I would face on my journey toward ordination; racism was alive and well. Rev. Richardson died in 1995, a few months after my ordination as deacon, and Ann died a year later.

At the time I started my ordination process, there were two ordinations—first as deacon, then as elder. I continued with the process with little to no support. I eventually was recruited by a large, urban, multicultural church in Minnesota as an associate pastor. They were seeking an African American woman as a part of their ministry team.

I moved to Minnesota in June of 1997 to begin the position. I was not allowed to have the associate pastor's office because the previous person, who no longer worked for the church, was allowed to keep it. Hmm, now that was strange. During my brief stay at the church, I faced challenges on every front. I was asked to schedule the Sunday evening worship for the remainder of the year. I completed a schedule for six months with speakers, music, visual and performing artists, only to have the senior pastor accuse me of being too assertive, and it could not have been done right since it only took a short time.

When I interviewed for the position, I was wearing my hair in braids, and I wore a kente cloth garment with my suit. I didn't want there to be any confusion as to how I present myself. Can you believe, an older African American woman in the congregation came to me and told me, "Some of the women in the congregation are upset about the way you dress and your hair, and your breasts are too big." Now, that was a bit too much, and, yes, I did respond to her—with love and kindness. Well, at least with love!

And then there were the complaints by the senior pastor that I was baptizing too many babies on Sundays, and could I please stop asking about praying for the sick during worship. He explained to me, "We don't talk about sad things during worship." But I did notice that rule didn't apply to affluent members of the congregation.

But these weren't the gut-wrenching things. I spent a lot of my time counseling women of the congregation who were being battered, parents who were being asked to leave the church because of the lifestyle choices of their children, and women dismayed by the racism and sexism. All of this from a congregation touted as being so "We are the world; we are the people." Things finally hit the fan when God gave me a message to preach from John 8:1–12, the passage about the woman accused of adultery, a message for a congregation that had piled up many stones to throw at others, yet never reflected upon itself.

By August, I was forced out of the congregation. I was told I could not enter the building or have any contact with the people. I was told to get out of my apartment, and my salary was being discontinued. I can't tell you what it is like for someone to tell you that you are not allowed to enter a church. But I knew that there were people in the congregation who had been treated the same.

Oh, you might say that I should have just not said anything. I should have ignored the message given to me by God. But it was God who brought me there, and it was God who would take care of me. A messenger of sorts was dispatched by the powers-that-be to tell me, "There's no place for you here in Minnesota so you should leave and go back to Missouri." I explained to the messenger that while I would love to leave, God had not told me to go anywhere, and so I remained.

Eventually the national offices of the denomination investigated the situation and it was determined that racism and sexism were rampant. I did not seek legal redress or compensation for the trauma. Since that time, at least two other African American associate pastors have come and gone from that congregation, under less than congenial circumstances, in less than seven years. The senior pastor is still there. "How I got over, how I got over, my Lord. My soul looks back and wonders, how I got over, my Lord."

This is only a brief glimpse into my story. In order to make it through, I had to rely on all of the resources God makes available. I had friends and family for support. I told them in detail about what I was going through, and my anguish. Keeping it a secret would not have given them a chance to live out their faith and minister to me at a time when I needed it most. Yes, I am a person of great faith, but I was in my Gethsemane, and I needed them. I had many sistah and brother friends who listened to my tear-filled cries late in the midnight hours, those who listened as I told my story over, and over again, and then over and over again. I remember very vividly one afternoon sitting in the middle of my bed so very depressed about what was going on as I tried to pack my things to leave my apartment. It felt as if a big sinkhole was opening and I was just about to drop through. Then a human angel was dispatched to my assistance. For more than two hours, by car phone, she played music and talked to me about God's goodness and my worthiness. As long as I live, I will never forget that afternoon.

I went into therapy to work through the hurt and pain. Don't let anyone tell you that therapy does not have value. I was fortunate enough to find a pastoral therapist who understood the context of my circumstances.

Last but not least, I am living well. Living well is a form of resistance to oppression. A good sista-friend, Rev. Gloria Roach Thomas, always tells me, "Just live well, Sista. Live well." By living well, I am referring to the art- and faith-filled resolution to not let a bad situation determine your destiny or outcome. Let God take care of the crazies and just go on with the plan God has for your life. In Psalm 110 it says "Sit at my right hand until I make your enemies your footstool."

At all times and in all places, I am continually in awe and wonder about what my God can do. I was blessed to become part of the ministry team at a healthy and thriving church, Wayman African Methodist Episcopal, where Rev. Dr. Alphonse Reff is the senior pastor. I went back to school and completed my doctorate of education in Critical Pedagogy, and I served as a scholar-in-residence, and assistant professor at the College of St. Catherine. While there, I conducted the Sankofa Project: Educating and Fostering Resilience in African-American Adolescent Girls, a womanist theological research project.

I was able to utilize my position to call together an assortment of brilliant, beautiful, bodacious black women from cross-sections of community, church, and academia for a two-year "Womanist Gathering." The results are being compiled into book format for the posterity of our future generations. We must network with each other and make the alliances with others who are willing to work with us on the behalf of liberation, and we must include our brothers of all races and colors who advocate for the elimination of violence toward women.

My position and my location has changed, but my commitment to the continuing work with women remains steadfast. Today, I serve as associate dean at Christian Theological Seminary in Indianapolis, Indiana. I'm just so very glad that I held onto God's unchanging hands!

My Sista, place your hand in God's hand, have faith, and stand on God's promises. Know that in whatever challenges you face in ministry, God will take care of you!

16 ᑐ IS THERE A BALM?
The Call to Urban Ministry

La Sandra Melton-Dolberry

Nondenominational

I am only one, but I am one. I cannot do everything but I can do something.
What I can do, that I ought to do, and what I ought to do, by the grace of
God I will do.

—Adam Clayton Powell,
Congressional Record,
February 18, 1965

My name is La Sandra Melton-Dolberry. I am the founder and pastor of Harambee Urban Ministries, which houses the Gathering Place Christian Fellowship, Harambee Family Resource Center, the Ladies of Perpetual Praise Dance Ensemble, and several other ministries. This year, I celebrate my twenty-sixth year in ministry.

When asked whom do I pastor, my answer is "the community." Though there is a specific group of folks who call me pastor, there are many more who have embraced me as such—primarily those who have been estranged from the traditional church setting. Nevertheless, they are clear that they desire direction and a closer walk with God. They can cite God as any of the clichés that we hear around the faith community. Some of them don't know what to call this All-Seeing, All-Knowing Deity. They simply identify the source as God.

The meaning of Harambee is from Swahili, "Let's get together and push." We interpret that as P.U.S.H!: Pray/Praise until Something Happens. We do a little more at Harambee in that we work for the community. We do whatever our hands find to do as unto God. We make sandwiches and feed the homeless, we collect clothing for those who are re-entering the workplace, but our chief concern is connecting folks to the Healer, the Attorney, the Great

Physician. We tend first to their practical needs so that they might focus on the spiritual.

Prior to my husband's retirement from the Army, for twenty-two years I traveled as a military wife. I always knew when it was time to get orders to relocate. I would get this immense desire to start taking pictures off the wall. It felt crazy, but sure enough usually in a couple of weeks, a month at the most, Dolberry would come in and say, "We got orders." "I knew it!" I would exclaim, "I just knew it!" Then the excitement would begin, the expectation would rise and we could start the detachment process from where we were.

It has been the same in the pulpit for me. One day God said to me, "I'm processing your orders. It's time for you to start releasing your positions here."

I was at a church I watched grow from having a close-knit family atmosphere to being a large congregation. They had taught me much, had been a great instrument for God to work some kinks out in me, and gave me the opportunity to use my spiritual gifts and all of my creative tools. I was able to be instrumental in the birthing of several ministries there.

It was not always peaches and cream, but these folks were excited and expectant, so with a little convincing, the sky could be the limit. Now it was time to leave. I started with giving up the Dance, Drama, and Drill program. The young adult ministry, which was my heart (though the credit was given to a brother), was one of the hardest ministries to release. We had fun, we had drama, we had debate, for these young people were curious, militant, and strong-willed, and it made for great ministry. Now I was being told to give them up. So I did. Next was the Children's Church. This ministry was as equally hard to release, but I realized it was not my baby. "Some plant, some water . . ." Last, but not least, was my ministry as praise and worship leader. When I came to the church, they knew nothing of praise and worship. They would do devotion. The pastor (at that time) called me a fireball and introduced me to the church. He had asked me beforehand to introduce the people to praise and worship. That's exactly what I did. They were more comfortable calling it a Songfest, but it was on! We graduated to having two worship teams, five choirs, and a praise and worship leader. I was able to convene a conference, which utilized many gifts for the worship of a Worthy God.

Well, leave I did. It was hard, but God's final word to me was "Get up and get out!" It was hard to leave what I knew and what was comfortable. I had a full music ministry at my disposal. All I had to do was walk out on the platform. The sound person knew everything about me. The minister of music knew my pitch and key. It was a piece of cake to lead the people of God into worship. Needless to say, as I started the transition, I was floundering. Where should I go? With whom will I be able to have fellowship? What will I do?

Then God said to me, "I really have enough people inside the walls preaching, teaching, singing and fellowshipping with each other. I need those who will take off their fine clothes, put down their briefcases for a minute, go out into the trenches, roll up their sleeves, and get their hands dirty for me. I need someone to "Take the church *to* the people!" I finally gave God my "Yes." This was the beginning of Harambee.

I first started with a group called SisterCircles. It was church for women exclusively. It was necessary, for it was a place that would allow any woman to come "as is." My pitch was "Come share your challenges, your struggles, your questions and your burdens." And come they did. We would sing, pray, and do rituals that brought healing. We did hand washing and circle ceremonies. We gave away trinkets as they came in the door. Sometimes it was flowers. At some point in our evening, usually the beginning, we would introduce ourselves with our flowers. We became the beautiful bouquet representing the SisterCircles of the world. Women were healed, liberated, birthed, and returned to their families more whole.

Then came the teens. Street Teens is what they called themselves. They were young people who attended (or, should I say, would not attend) their alternative school. They were thugs, hookers, gang-bangers, thieves, hoods . . . you name it. I was requested by the principal and the head counselor to come to the school. My title was Joint Diploma counselor, but what I really did was meet the youth, where they were, and minister to them "on the down low." The program did facilitate a means for them to receive a much coveted high school diploma. It also meant a program of discipline for a group of kids who had not known structure. We utilized a grant from tobacco (written by the district counselor, Lorraine Johnson), which was intended for a school newsletter. The response was so great, it eventually evolved into the newspaper. It was not easy. I was not dealing with easy kids. But I met them where they were. "You have a second chance," I told them. "But don't play with me. If you're not serious, don't waste your time or mine and don't waste the taxpayer's money." I designed for each of them a structured program that obligated them to attend school two days more than required. They rose to the challenge!

I watched these kids evolve. They would sit in our bungalow after school hours and dialogue about the "craziness" they had lived through and were living in. They were Latino, Somalian, Ethiopian, African American, Caucasian, and Filipino. Most of all they were family. They facilitated a forum between the head gang-leaders and the San Diego Police Department on neutral turf. They were amazing. But first we had to deal with their woundedness, their pain, their challenges, their questions, and their immediate needs. They became the healers of their families, visionaries of their communities, and carriers of the Word of God.

We lost one teenaged boy. His name was Jesse and he fell through the cracks of the systems. Jesse was a victim, and he was overwhelmed at home. I would hear from him when he had run away from home. We would always schedule time to meet and talk, but Jesse would never come. Eventually I saw him on the six o'clock news. He had killed a boy and dumped his body. He was our one casualty.

But graduation day came and Santana, who came to us at the age of thirteen as a domestic violence victim, was our valedictorian. Her GPA had risen from 0.8 to 3.6. I was their pastor, the only one they had known. Our hook was the newspaper. They covered the Super Bowl here in the city and their self-esteem went straight through the roof. They had press passes and camera equipment, and the "real" press treated them as colleagues. Our day never began without sharing and never ended without prayer. Jesus was our Chief Editor, on the down low of course. Today I watch those young people who are adults negotiate on adult terms. Santana acknowledged a call to preach. I would find her in cemeteries talking to gang-members. She is now the champion of her family, the only one to graduate from high school, and working as the secretary to a bank president. We are still in relationship.

My last public clergy position was that of chaplain to San Diego's Children's Center. This was a residential center for abused, abandoned, and displaced children—the kids who are mostly forgotten once they are behind the walls. It is easy to forget and to overlook them. Some of these kids sang in church choirs, served on Junior Usher Boards, and attended Sunday school in Your Church, USA. Some never had the luxury to do so. They do not run in the halls or congregate in the vestibule. Community Church for them is out of reach, foreign, and not part of their lives. But in this place, the Sunday morning church service has become the breathing space they not only get to congregate in, but also where they look for some sign that they are still significant on this sphere. Many suspect they are being lied to, but even a good lie renders hope in the face of desperation. They are fed a steady diet of meds to prevent them from expressing their pain, acting out, and thinking too much. They are given a license to be "crazy." After all, they have reasons to be. At eighteen they are dismissed.

It took the entire year to convince "the powers that be" that it was necessary to tend to the "whole" child. Not just their psyches, not just their physical bodies, not just their emotions. Many of them were wounded and violated spiritually as well, some by spiritual leaders whom they trusted. As these children began to change, the psychologists took note and began to consult me with each case. It doesn't mean that I had a phone booth and a cape! About many of them I could only pray. But many of them got a new beginning simply by me giving them Hope: Hope who forgives, Hope who restores, Hope who washes, and Hope who loves. The administration had brought me onboard to kill that Sunday service. I would not and could not do that. I did offer to call in a priest for the Catholics (none identified) and an imam for the Muslims, but I could not and would not kill the Christian service. Every one of you knows the children in this story. Their names may change, but their souls, their longings, their experiences are the same

At the end of my turn, my call was to come out of a place that was steeped in politics and bureaucracy. It had become very clear to me that these children were only minimally treated, by design. It was a matter of money and it was heart breaking. I decided to come out and use what I'd learned to prevent families, children, *and* the people who love them from having to enter that system. I returned to my own group of ministries and community, working even more diligently for the people I served the parents, the children and all the people who love them. We have been able to prevent many families from going into that system. I do not have the time or space to tell you about them, but it is an awesome task and it's a humble walk. Urban ministry as I know it, is an excellent opportunity to become a bridge for the Almighty. For those who have not known and for those who have walked away from the body of Christ, the church, as well as for those who long to trust but need a community fellowship, I reach out as their bridge. I am reminded of the armless statue of Christ in front of one of the churches with the inscription, "I have no hands but yours." Harambee is not church as usual. It is not taking people to church; instead it is taking the church to the people. It's not giving a sermon as much as being a sermon. It requires me allowing God to put God's "Super" to my "natural." It means becoming a channel, an instrument, and a willing vessel for the realm of God. "Know ye not that your body is the temple of the Holy Ghost?" (1 Cor. 6:19 KJV). Well, I take that temple to the people!

I went on sabbatical at Boston University. I worked with three other female pastors to study the issue of the "stained glass ceiling" that confronts women in local congregations. This was a first-time experience in my entire ministry! I have learned that I have little left to give if I am burned out. Without good structure it is quite easy to become so in this vein of urban ministry. One must truly keep up with one's spiritual health, take time off, steal away, and replenish, for there is much work, but few laborers. I was firmly refreshed by this sisterhood and our research times and trips together. When the season was complete, I determined that I would return for another round of "refreshment" through sabbatical or for whatever else God has planned for me next.

Urban outreach ministry is an endless opportunity for people to see Jesus the Christ walking the streets. We leave off pious collars but wear jeans, shorts, slacks, whatever is conducive to the call of the day. Periodically, I serve in my robe, especially when it's communion worship or one of our collaborative gatherings. But dress does not define an urban minister. It's all about the relationships that we are forming in the name of Jesus Christ.

Urban pastors are not perfect and this is what usually draws people to someone like me. I wear dread-locks and plenty of African outfits and can speak the language of the streets. This gives others permission to come with their own brokenness, their hang-ups, their habits, their skeletons, and their questions. But I will be honest and say that there are times when "you must never let 'em see ya sweat." They look for champions. That's just the way it is. So it's always essential that I "represent"!

The revelation that has come for me is that the pinnacle of urban ministries is not building a megachurch. There are no walls that can contain it. Urban ministry is more like Mary's alabaster box! Urban ministry is designed to be deliberately and intentionally broken and poured out, over and over again. Instead of a fragrance that will fade with time, this precious box releases the reality of the Christ, the Anointed One and his Anointing. I know for certain and can say with assurance, *there is a balm in Gilead!*

Sage Wisdom *on*

Cross-Cultural Ministries

17 ∼ SISTA, YOU MUST PREACH!

Michelle R. Loyd-Paige

Nondenominational

And blessed is she who believed, for there will be a fulfillment of those things which were told her from the LORD.

—Luke 1:45 NKJV

Perhaps nothing more clearly demonstrates the problem of sexism than the fact that women are by far the majority of sexual assault victims. We live with a constant awareness that it could happen to us. That's why blaming the victim is a common response. According to psychologists, people do not want to acknowledge that they are vulnerable so they rationalize that an assault happened because of something the victim did or didn't do, instead of blaming a perpetrator for committing a crime.

—Lori S. Robinson, *I Will Survive*

When I think back to that one cool Saturday afternoon in the fall of 1984—the afternoon a woman of God prophesied over my life, saying, "Sister, you must preach"—I see, all the more clearly, that everything that has happened in my life since then has added to the richness of ministry that I now enjoy. But I had not always thought that this was the case. If I have learned anything along the way it would be this: like a game of double-dutch jump rope, it takes courage and timing to do ministry well, but most of all you have to believe!

When I first heard those words, "Sister, you must preach," I literally ran. I had not come to the "Be Still and Know" women's retreat to hear a word from God. I wasn't there to find my purpose or more clearly discern the call of God on my life. Ministry, purpose, and calling were the farthest things from my mind. No, I was there just to see what this "retreat" thing was all about . . . at least that is what I thought. I now understand that God was setting into motion the preparation for my life in ministry. It would be more than a year before I told my pastor or my husband what had happened at the retreat. It took that long for me to stop running from my purpose and to answer the call for God to preach the gospel. It would take more than a year for me to truly believe, not just the word of the prophetess, but also the Word of God to me.

Now, more than twenty years later (has it really been that long? It seems like only yesterday I heard those words that would so greatly impact my life), I am beginning my eighteenth year as a minister of the gospel and celebrating the fourth anniversary of my own ministry, Preach Sista! Inc. Preach Sista! Inc. is a ministry committed to equipping, maturing, and perfecting the body of Christ. We host several events annually: the PreachSista! Fresh Anointing Conference, which provides a platform for women to preach; the Time for Honor Banquet, which recognizes the ministry gifts women bring to the church; the Daughters of Thunder Preaching Series, which showcases the many gifts and styles of women in ministry; and the Preach Sista! Christmas Party, which hosts women from a local shelter. Soon, we will begin hosting a series of preaching workshops for women. All of these ministries stem from my most heartfelt desire and the mission of this ministry to embrace, encourage, and equip women of God for ministering to the whole body of Christ.

Pursuing ordination as a minister and founding a women's ministry that was not directly connected to an established church have been the raw materials of the life-in-ministry project God has been designing for me. At first, I was not excited about either. When I was in my late teens, my mother became a minister and through her experiences I had a front row seat to sexism in the church. She was verbally attacked, was prohibited from standing in the pulpit to preach, and spent long hours "in the service of the Lord" for very little financial compensation or consideration for her responsibilities at home as a wife and mother of four children still in school. All of this put a strain on the household and her relationship with my father. Why would I want to go through the same thing?

But something happened to me that cool fall afternoon so many years ago. I had an encounter with God. And though I tried to run away from the call to preach, literally and figuratively, there came a point in my life when I realized that I would find no true peace within myself until I surrendered my will to God's.

Surrendering to the will of God, answering the call to preach the gospel, and establishing a new ministry are more than just notions, as anyone who has done so will tell you. For me, all three actions took a great measure of courage, a keen understanding/discerning of God's timing, and the personal strength produced only from my believing in God.

COURAGE

"Have I not commanded thee? Be strong and of a good courage; be not afraid, neither be thou dismayed; for the LORD thy God is with thee withersoever you goest" (Josh. 1:9 KJV).

According to Webster's Dictionary, "courage" is the mental or moral strength to venture, persevere, and withstand danger, fear, or difficulty. Because of my mother's involvement in ministry, I was very much aware of the difficulty many women encounter when pursuing ordination. Resistance to women assuming positions of leadership and spiritual authority in the church may come from several places: one's denomination, one's pastor, one's family and friends, church members, complete strangers, and even from one's own mental "tapes" of self-doubt. Tradition is a formidable foe, especially, if it is the only thing that you have ever known.

It takes courage to say, "I believe God has called me to preach," when everything and everyone around you is saying, "God does not call women to preach." It takes mental strength to "count the costs" and still proceed down a chosen path all the while knowing that resistance and opposition is just around the corner. I have encountered resistance at many points along my journey to where I am today. My first encounter did not come from my pastor; he was very supportive of my quest for ordination. It came from a dear sister in my congregation who pulled me aside after a service where I had preached the morning message and asked me, "Do you really think God has called you to preach? Do you think God would call a woman when there is a man available?" I told her, politely, to take it up with the One Who Called Me! "Pray about it and let me know what God said." The most hurtful comments came from a former pastor who suspected that I was starting Preach Sista! as a way to draw people from the congregation and to start my own church. The most surprising resistance came from my brother-in-law. He loves me, but was (and still is) convinced that women should not be ministers or pastors. Women can be Sunday school teachers maybe, but not clergy. He even tried to show me passages in his Bible that he believes confirms his believe that God did not want women in church leadership. You know the passages. I took his Bible and showed him examples of where God did use women to proclaim the Word of God and lead nations. It takes courage to withstand the questioning of one's calling. Yes, it takes courage to face resistance from without, but even more courage to face the resistance that comes from one's own mind.

Partly as a form of self-protection, partly as a response to the lack of female role models, and partly because we do not really know who we are or what we are capable of, our minds sometimes go into overdrive trying to persuade our souls that "God could not be calling us into ministry." Our minds cry out, "There must have been a misunderstanding somewhere" from deep within our inner selves. "After all," our inside voice continues, "I didn't ask for this. This is not what I signed up for! This is not my answer to prayer."

My inner struggles took the form of an acute awareness of my lack of seminary training, my lack of financial resources, and my reluctance to see myself as a leader. In my early years in ministry, I earnestly believed that I had been called to preach, but where and how? Would anyone see me as qualified? Would anyone open the pulpit to me, a woman? Could my husband, who was becoming increasingly intolerant of the hypocrisy found in local churches, stand being married to a minister—after all, when we married with children, I had no plans to be a preacher! I stressed myself out almost to the breaking point with these questions that came not from others, but from my own mind. But day by day, I learned that it takes courage to answer the call into ministry not knowing fully where you are headed or the exact price you will have to pay. Day by day I learned what it meant to be courageous, in spite of myself.

TIMING

"But they that wait upon the LORD shall renew their strength; they shall mount up with wings as eagles; they shall they shall run, and not be weary; and they shall walk, and not faint" (Isa. 40:31 KJV).

Timing, according to Webster, is the "selection for maximum effect of the precise moment for beginning or doing something."

"Timing is everything," can be often heard in boardrooms across the nation. It is essential that a business expansion plan is properly executed, that a new product is introduced at the height of the latest craze, and that stock shares are sold at their highest value. In business timing is everything. And while timing may not be everything in ministry it is a very important part. No one wants to miss the "due season" or "time of visitation." But like Sarah, we may get impatient with the pace of the fulfillment of God's Word to us. We run ahead of God and we end up with a Hagar and Ishmael in our lives. Timing in ministry is based upon our being spiritually ready for the tasks God has prepared for us, the people we are to minister to being ready to receive us, and our being willing and available to carry out the work of the ministry.

About eight years into my service at the church that held my ordination credentials, I was beginning to feel like I was lagging behind "everybody else." So I asked God why, if I'd been called to preach, was I not preaching more? God's response humbled me to my core. "You are not yet ready!" Yes, I was called to preach and I would be preaching more when the timing was right. We were going to work on God's timetable, not mine. I spent the next two years more intently studying the Word of God. I wrote many sermons, even when I knew I had no place to preach them. All I knew was that when God said , "It's your time, Michelle," I was going to be ready.

During this waiting season I lived by the scripture "Study to show thyself approved" (2 Tim. 2:15 KJ21). During this waiting season my skills were honed, my discernment of God's voice sharpened, my understanding of ministry broadened, and my time available to travel increased. After those two years, I began preaching more. The founding of Preach Sista! Inc. would come five years later. Had I been impatient and unwilling to wait on God's timing for doors to be opened to speak or for the establishment of my own ministry for women, I would have either given up and pursued a career in the secular business world or ventured down a ministry path called "Ishmael." Timing is not everything in ministry but it is essential to carrying out God's purpose and plans for our lives.

BELIEVING

"But without faith it is impossible to please God: for [she] that cometh to God must believe that God is, and that God is a rewarder of them that diligently seek God" (Heb. 11:6 KJV).

Believing, according to Webster's, is "to accept trustfully and on faith; to have a firm conviction as to the reality or goodness of something." When it comes to ministry, sometimes the hardest thing to do is to just keep believing that what God has spoken is actually going to come to pass. Many times I have wanted to "see first" and then believe. But, more often than not, God wanted me to believe first and then watch for the fulfillment of the promise. The founding of Preach Sista! is a good example.

When I felt it impressed upon me to launch Preach Sista! my circumstances were far from ideal. I had taken a 50 percent pay cut on my job, and what savings I had were designated to cover the half of my income I had lost! Big visions take big money and I had none to spare. My home church was struggling to recover from a split and some had assumed that Preach Sista! was an attempt to start my own church. It was not and some people were disappointed that I didn't plant a new church and others simply didn't trust me completely. Friends—you know, the ones who say "I'm with you, whatever you need just call"— those friends who had always supported my preaching were nowhere to be found when it came to organizing, promoting, and attending our first events. When I asked God what was going on, "Did I not hear your voice, was it just my imagination? 'Cause things are not looking too good," all I heard in response was, "Will you trust me? Will you still believe in spite of what you see and feel?"

Preach Sista! lost over three thousand dollars that first year! It was tempting to stop believing. But I could not afford to not believe God. Yes, people disappointed me and I stopped believing in some people. I could even stop believing in myself for a moment, but not believe God? That was a different story. I had to believe God! If I couldn't trust God when I heard, "Now is the time to launch Preach Sista!" how could I have trusted God when I was called to preach? I chose to believe God and now, almost five years later, Preach Sista! is operating in the black. We are now incorporated and have 501c3 status.

We still encounter challenges, but every challenge is an opportunity to believe God more. I do not think that believing God is the same thing as having unshakable faith. I don't think any one that is human is truly unshakable. Being shaken is a sign of our humanity. God knows how we are made. Tests and trials will come. And, as they say, "That which doesn't kill you will make you stronger." The trick is not to live in the doubts that cause us to shake.

One way to not be ensnared by our own doubts is to be ever mindful of what we do believe. One way that I do this is to recite my own "statement of faith" on a regular basis. Almost every morning, I end my time of prayer with these words:

> I believe the Word of God and I believe my God will do what God has promised, for God cannot lie! My path is growing brighter and brighter as I stay with God's perfect plan. Even now God's Word is being fulfilled through me and in me. Daily I will continue to seek God's face. I will not give in to fear, doubt, or despair. I thank you, Adoni, that you are able to keep that which I have committed to You. And so I say, God my provider, regarding this prayer, I shall not be moved. I have believed, therefore have I spoken and I shall continue to speak until I see the full manifestation. In Jesus' name, I pray. Amen.

Twenty years ago I heard God speaking to me through the voice of a woman. Though I had tried to run from the call, I found no true peace until I started running with the call. I was not one of those sisters who always knew and always wanted to be in ministry. No, I was sure that, vocationally, I was going to be in either the business world or in the medical field, almost anything but proclaiming the gospel as a vocation. But since I have accepted this high calling, God has allowed me to take all my experiences, all my hopes, all my fears, all my insecurities, all my training, all my accomplishments, all my gifts, all my pain, all my joy—all of who I am—to embrace, encourage, and equip women who are answering the call to ministry, because I dared to believe the word from God that was given me.

Linda H. Hollies

United Methodist Church

Theological investigation into the experiences of Christian Black women reveals that Black women consider the Bible to be a major source for religious validation in their lives. Though Black women's relationship with God preceded their introduction to the Bible, this Bible gave some content to their God-consciousness. The source for Black women's understanding of God has been twofold: first, God's revelation directly to them, and, second, God's revelation as witnessed in the Bible and as read and heard in the context of their experience. The understanding of God as Creator, sustainer, comforter, and liberator took on life as they agonized over their pain, and celebrated the hope that as God delivered the Israelites, they would be delivered as well. The God of the Old and New Testament became real in the consciousness of oppressed Black women. Though they were politically impotent, they were able to appropriate certain themes of the Bible which spoke to their reality."

—Jacquelyn Grant, *White Women's Christ and Black
Women's Jesus: Feminist Christology and Womanist Response*

Just as I was getting ready to graduate from seminary, my mother died! It was an unexpected death and my grief was overwhelming. I began to seek the face of God about how to make it through this new season. Very clearly I heard God say to "call for your sisters in ministry." Without hesitation, I began to invite clergy women from around the area to meet with me at the Michigan State University continuing education site, the Kellogg Center, in Lansing, Michigan. More than seventy-five women responded to my invitation.

We gathered to worship. We divided into small groups. I asked girlfriends to facilitate workshops in their areas of ministry. We reached out to each other with our shared wisdom, our comfort, and our support. At the conclusion of our first "Advance: A Time for Women to Grow Forward," the question began to surface, "Can we do this again?"

The date was set for the next year, and the next. In about the third year, one of the members of the local planning team, Betty Quinney, who worked for the state of Michigan, offered to do the paperwork of incorporation for the ministry. We registered as a nonprofit incorporation with the intent of using seminary trained women to teach non-seminary trained women what we had learned. This year we begin our twenty-first year of ministry and have become a nonprofit 501c3, with the same educational focus. The need has not lessened among women for training, counseling, and educational support. It has increased as more women seek different avenues for expressing their passion and purpose within God's realm.

I was inspired to call our annual gatherings Advance. As a group that was primarily women of African descent, I knew that we could not afford to "retreat"! We had to move full steam ahead and work with diligence in order to catch up with the rest of a changing world. Most of us belonged to the black church, which did not easily recognize women in pastoral leadership. Many of us were lay women who wanted knowledge and support as they sought to work in their church areas. We tried to include "whosoever" wanted to attend. Our numbers began to swell and our excitement about possibilities grew.

It was my mother's death that sent me looking for other women who could walk with me during a stressful period. I needed comfort, support, and care. I needed another woman to understand my grief, not judge my tears and share with me the words of wisdom that had brought her through a death experience. I needed someone to sing for me when I could not sing. I longed for someone to pray for me when I could not pray. I needed a safe place to speak my truth, my pain, and my turmoil at not understanding a God who took away and did not give! The women who came were my healing links. They brought me balm for my wounds. At the beginning, I was only a "voice in the wilderness" crying out for help and for solace. I cannot explain what the gathering of sisters did for my soul.

Many of the original group of women have remained steadfast sister-friends over the years. We have moved across the country. Our life stories have changed and evolved. Often we do more e-mailing than talking. We no longer host an annual event. Yet we are a continuing support group, clearinghouse, enablers of one another, and we are collaborators one of another. Our largest gathering was held at Clark University, where we hosted more than four hundred women from twenty-one different denominations. The gathering was called I Have an Appointment! It was an urgent time in all of our lives.

There are no words to describe, explain, or detail the awesome wonder of a gathering of women from around the world who come together for the express purpose of worshiping, learning, sharing, eating, laughing, and caring for one another. We were intentional about building new networks. Being hosted by Clark University in Atlanta, we lived in their brand new four-plex dorms, met in their auditorium, and ate in their cafeteria. Each dorm was assigned a hostess-facilitator who was a seminary graduate. Each night the women in that dorm met together to rehearse their day, to voice their questions, and to seek clarity for their emerging dreams, hopes, and visions.

Every morning began with an hour of prayer, led by Rev. Dr. Jeannette Chandler-Kotey, who is currently director of music ministries for First Baptist Church in Birmingham, Alabama. There were only music and prayers. It was a rich and powerful experience to set the tone for the rest of our day. We had a morning plenary and utilized the variety of denominational women to teach and to preach. There were workshops in the afternoon, with free time. A nightly worship with a special preacher featured musicians and dancers, who set the stage for worship. A black Catholic religious, Rev. Mother of Chicago, brought the house down! Our last keynote preacher, Rev. Dr. Brenda J. Little, the very first black Baptist woman to be ordained, sent us home with a lesson in the art of fighting for what we wanted.

During our preplanning stage we met with Rev. Barbara King, in her new multimillion-dollar facility, built in the round. She invited us, welcomed us, and helped us to host our opening night worship there. She agreed to become our keynote speaker at the banquet and shared her story of strength and power in ministry with us, along with the pain, disappointments, and frustrations. Yet she stood, tall and regal, and we saw the evidence of years of her labor come to fruition. As clergy women marched to the sound of an African drum, robed in their regalia, it was a mystical, magical, and magnificent moment to behold! Each one of us had an appointment with the Divine! We met to share the mystery of our common journey. We left refreshed.

I cannot give you the cause of God telling me to "let go." I cannot offer you the specific words that spoke to my spirit saying this was my "farewell" to conferences. All that I can say was that God moved me away from hostessing events of this nature at the conclusion of this stellar event. Talk about pain. It was almost as bad as the grief of losing my mother! Yet, I clearly heard God speak and I obeyed. The next year God gave me the opportunity to call together many of the participants to assist in writing *The Sister to Sister Journal,* volume 2, which was published by Judson Press. This bestselling work focused on some aspect of the healing each one of us had received on our journey. The Rev. Dr. Susan Johnson-Cook had edited the first volume of the book, and she has gone on to do even greater things than she imagined in her ministry. She was the first female clergy to be elected president of the Hampton Minister's Conference of more than ten thousand black Baptist pastors! This was certainly a major appointment.

Some of the original women who helped to establish Woman to Woman Ministries, Inc. are Rev. Beverly Garvin, AME of Livonia, Michigan; Rev. DaisyBelle Thomas-Quinney, Church of God/ Anderson, of Montgomery, Alabama; Rev. Dr. Eleanor L. Miller, Baptist, of Chicago, Illinois; Rev. Dr. Florida Morehead, nondenominational, of Fort Hood, Maryland; Rev. Lucille Jackson, AME, of Maywood, Ill.; Rev. Geraldine Black, UMC, of Chicago, Illinois; Rev. Terrill Cistrunk, Presbyterian, of Milwaukee, Wisconsin; and Rev. Elizabeth Garcia, COGIC, of Lansing, Michigan. Also included in our first Advance, was our size two, powerful preaching sister, the Rev. Janet Hopkins, UMC, of Chicago, Illinois, who is now deceased and greatly missed.

The journey of Woman to Woman began with a death and continued to turn and twist and take a different venue with the death of my parish ministry and then the death of my youngest son, Grelon Renard Everett. Death seems to be a moving and motivating metaphor for birth within my life! For I refuse to be taken down for the count by a natural life occurrence! However, it was not my "natural" inclination to stay up and keep fighting. It was the call of two sisters who pushed me to take another journey with this ministry. After being put on a leave of absence by my bishop due to the racism within my appointment, I began to wrestle with major depression. I was facing the death of my professional career. I felt that this was "the end" for me. I went to bed, sort of a modern day time of being in sackcloth and ashes! However, I was not repenting, but lamenting.

One night Rev. Michelle Cobb and Rev. Ida Easley, both seminary classmates from Garrett Evangelical Theological Seminary, double-teamed me on a conference call.

They allowed me to cry, to vent, and to make excuses for being in bed on my private couch. Then they challenged my happy behind! "Linda, God moved you from a place. God did not take away your gifts. What do you need in this time period of your life?" I wanted and needed a quiet, calming space. I needed somewhere near water. I needed a place where talking was not mandatory and tears were honored as prayers. I needed the comfort of my sisters, who would understand my pain, not judge me, but support me without me having to explain. Their direct mandate was, "Go and build it!" Then, they both sent me their personal funds to assist with finding and establishing WomanSpace, a Center for God's Bodacious Women.

WomanSpace was a four-room loft in the heart of downtown Grand Rapids, across the street from the Grand River. Mista Chuck, my spouse, Grian, my daughter, my biological sisters, Jackie Brodie Davis and Regina Pleasant, and their respective spouses, Robert Davis and Riene Adams-Morris, all came to assist with the grand opening of this sacred space. The beautiful ambiance spoke "tranquility." The constantly falling water in a reservoir Mista Chuck designed and built spoke "refreshing." A reading area, gathering space, study tables, healing chair, and gallery of women's artwork, books, and magazines spoke, "Come and be awhile."

It was a gathering space. It was a calming space. It was a counseling place. And it was a healing space. I became a spiritual director, a group facilitator, and an individual pastoral counselor, for my sisters called me out of depression and back into full time ministry, woman to woman!

I thought that this was my final stop in ministry. I felt that this was my destination. I felt secure at WomanSpace. And, again, God called, "Move." Mista Chuck and I had to pack up WomanSpace. A girlfriend, Dr. Paulette Sankofa, said, "Make WomanSpace portable, pack it in tubs, and take it where you go." She was a prophet! We did pack our "stuff and things" in huge tubs. I sold most of the furniture to another sister, Kim McCovery, a licensed social worker, who was just venturing out to begin her ministry of Living Water, a ministry to women coming from prison seeking reunification with their children. We brought all of our tubs and the water fountain, pillows, and the prayer chair with us to Calvary Church in Jackson, Michigan. God had prepared a chapel in this huge facility that was being underutilized. In December of 2006, a Sacred Space for Prayer was dedicated to the glory of God and the people of our community!

Woman to Woman Ministries, Inc. is alive and well. We just keep on keeping on doing the ministry of equipping women with educational, inspirational, and motivational information. To our God be all the glory, honor, and praise!

19 ∾ PERSISTENT, PERSEVERING, AND PRESENT

Angela Taylor Perry

Reformed Church

Womanist Wisdom says: Follow your own path. Many times you will walk alone, it will seem. But you are actually never alone. For Jesus has promised to never leave you or to forsake you. The poem "Footprints" has been carried to an extreme in many instances. But its reality is worth taking note of when we feel forsaken. For when we take a step and walk into places where "fools dare not tread," it is there that we will be carried. Because we must go through! There is no easy way to our divine destiny. The bumps are what lift us to higher heights.

—Linda H. Hollies, *Bodacious Womanist Wisdom*

There were once abolitionists and segregationists, perhaps even desegregationists. Who am I? I am an *integrationist*! I have come to discover that the essence of being an integrationist is persistence, perseverance, and presence. I am indeed this and more; a twenty-year triumphant survivor of multiple sclerosis, African American, over fifty and a "sold out" believer in the living resurrected, reconciling power of God through Jesus Christ! The question I really want to answer for you is how a physically challenged black woman could become so certain that she was called to gather and integrate individuals of differing ethnic and racial make-ups into a ministry. It's a pretty awesome reality for me and all I encounter.

I already stated that an integrationist must be persistent, persevering, and present. The question becomes how my presence is necessary for the spiritual formation of racial reconciliation in the Christian Reformed Church, a denomination founded by Dutch immigrants from the Netherlands in the late 1800s. Yes, the Dutch folk were the first to bring Africans to America! I guarantee that this story won't be colored through rose-colored glasses. This story will be colored and shaded by God's desire to take a broken and tainted Sistergirl and mold her into becoming a broken, living vessel for the edification of the church and the glory of God.

Before I illumine your minds on what I believe God is calling me to proclaim for racial reconciliation in the church, I should like to invite you into my journey and into my heart.

I grew up in a small, rural farm town in southwest Michigan, Cassopolis! That's just five miles up the road from the Underground Railroad. It's been said that the town is known for beautiful, light-skinned, black women, one of the rich consequences of slavery. The closest house to the left and to the right of our farmhouse was at least a mile away. When I was in early elementary school I was bussed with other black kids to a little country school at least ten miles from home. When I was in the third grade I dreaded going to recess because this tall, blonde, skinny white boy managed to get me in the corner of the gym every day, so he could lean down in my face and call me "little nigger girl." He terrified me; I suppose that was his intent.

At this same elementary school, I remember a circle of little white girls singing and pretending they were the Beatles. I remember that I was always standing outside the circle watching them play, watching them jump rope, and never being invited to join the circle. There was no one like me in the school, so I just watched them. It seemed normal to me. One rainy day right before recess the school principal played the local radio station over the intercom. President Kennedy had been assassinated. A cloud of sadness filled the room. When the bell rang I followed the white girls out to the playground (my usual experience). I can't remember how it all happened. It all happened so fast. One little girl with a quick lip and a shrill voice started screaming and said that I had thrown a big rock on her foot. The next thing I knew I was called to come inside. As soon as I passed through the double doors the school principle grabbed me by my hair and pulled me limping down the hall. She hurt me! I suddenly felt frightened, alone, and unprotected. Never had I felt such fear. I thought my teachers were my protectors. She forced me to sit down on a hard chair in her office and started to question me about why I would do such a thing. I remember now that she was angry with me because I was silent. I was too scared to speak. After that I learned to fear white female teachers.

I grew up as an only child with two faithful canine companions. Not long after my thirteenth birthday the little neighbor girl that I had played with every summer came and told me we had the same mother. I was in shock! This meant that we were sisters. It was a confusing dilemma to discover that the mother I knew was really my great aunt. When I was fourteen my aunt orchestrated my signing my own adoption papers. That's a whole different chapter.

During high school I was forbidden to hang out with the "black girls." They could come over to my house and play but I could not go over to their house. I could, however, go ten miles away and stay overnight with one little blonde-haired Sandy. We were in 4-H together. Our project was obedience dog training. Can you imagine that, a little black girl competing at dog shows! I was actually very good. I never understood why my mother was so passive regarding our own race. I grew up lacking cultural identity and racial awareness. I didn't think I was white but I certainly was not aware of my blackness. In my early twenties I wrote this poem to express the warring in my soul. I call it "Echoes of a Voice":

Oh what an experience
I feel cheated of my blackness
I feel anger
ENVY
almost hate for the white in me
I want to holler at my mother
she was doing her best
Her best
but not my best
what was best?
I am angry because I can see the Black in me
I can't feel the Black in me
and to think that one time
I took pride in not sounding Black
now my heart bleeds to be free of this
white façade
all her faces
Will the real me stand up!
Stand up and be counted among the rest
not set apart, labeled

for what
My ego is not in vain
only my pride
but which one
the Black or the White?
My heart cries out to my many brothers and sisters
who were forced in their ignorance
to become somebody
but who?
We are not White or are we?
We look Black, we sound white
We look
out of Black faces through white perspectives
Somewhere deep in our souls we find the rhythm
We hear the drum
We rock on the beat
yet something is missing
Something that doesn't allow us to fit
black or white
so who the hell are we?
help us . . . we hurt

My desire to be an advocate for racial reconciliation and cultural integration, particularly in the Christian Reformed Church, began in 1987 five years after I experienced three major spinal fusions and one year after I was diagnosed with multiple sclerosis. These traumas had the potential to anger me but instead they liberated me to pick up my own personal cross and to march forward boldly for change. Here are two incidents that have spurred me on.

One afternoon while preparing for my three young children to come home from school, I received a phone call from a Christian Reformed youth leader with a request for my children to be recipients of a high school youth group project. It was Christmas time and they wanted to adopt a family through giving. It sounded like a good opportunity for fellowship to me so I said yes. They asked me to make a list of my children's clothes sizes and their gift wishes. I was a single, welfare mom who stayed prayed-up. I trusted God through my circumstances and every now and then we were richly blessed. This phone call seemed an answer to our prayers. My children and I anticipated the young people in our home with excitement. We were prepared to greet them with intentional hospitality.

The group came with gift-wrapped boxes of clothes, shoes, and toys. They filled the kitchen table with bags of groceries, enough for a fine Christmas dinner. They decorated a real Christmas tree with an array of Christmas ornaments beyond our conception. There must have been at least twelve young people and three adults. Our house was festive. My children and I were looking forward to sharing cocoa, cookies, and conversation. The young people seemed to have had a silent good time decorating the tree and placing all the presents under it, *without* our help. The children and I just sat and watched. When they completed the task they shook our hands, wished us a Merry Christmas, smiled a bit, and left.

As they left the children tried to offer the treats that they prepared but were cordially refused. I can still see my children's bewildered faces. This could have been such a blessing in growth and fellowship for all of us. Instead, my thinking was about how shallow and used I felt because this event only perpetuated white paternalistic values.

Towards the end of that same year the Holy Spirit guided me into a vocal music ministry in worship services throughout Kalamazoo. From 1987 to 1995, I sang in nearly every Christian Reformed and Reformed Church in the Kalamazoo area. The first church I sang at was Hope Reformed. My vocal coach encouraged me to go as her substitute one Sunday morning. When I arrived at the church I quickly scanned the congregation for ethnic faces. There were none. While I was singing the pre-sermon selection I noticed that the people barely moved, smiled, or made eye contact. I was terrified. After I sang there was so much silence you could hear your own breathing. There was no clapping and no "amens" and definitely no "hallelujahs!" I thought I had sounded terrible. My anxiety reached a boiling point as I stepped to the pulpit to sing the post-sermon selection. Again there was no response. I sat down to my seat feeling embarrassed. After the service I was completely surprised when a flood of folk came intentionally forward to greet me and to tell me how blessed they were with my music. Applause was forbidden in this church.

I was surprised to receive return invitations there and from other area churches. I tolerated the silence after my singing and waited to accept their traditional response after the service. Through the years the greetings were predictable and the sincerity a bit quenched, yet I adapted to their culture and their blessings. On one return visit to the first church, a new thing happened. After the first song I heard about three or four isolated claps throughout the congregation. They didn't sound exactly rebellious; instead the claps had a deliberate ring to them. Preceding my singing of the post-sermon selection the pastor stood before his parishioners and said, "I noticed that some of you wanted to clap after Angela sang. I've decided that clapping is alright. I believe it is alright to show a singer appreciation and glory to God by applause." He sat down quietly. I sang again, and this time their applause was like an *explosion of praise* to God. That's how I perceived it. They were set free and so was I. The poem, "I Am" by Jordan Martin tells it better.

I AM

The day I became a swan
I stretched wide
my wings
arched my long willowy neck
and with my feet
firm on the ground
I made my statement
and said
I too
am a
Beautiful Black Queen
now
I can fly!

As my music ministry continued I began to witness a change that melted my heart and greeted my soul with divine purpose. When the flood of folk came up to greet me after services I saw Jesus in their eyes and when we were at arms length, we fell into an embrace that gave glory to God as we forgot about the color of skin. Moments like these were affirmation for this work that I do.

Racial reconciliation, racial harmony, racial justice, diversity training, and cultural sensitivity are words used across the United States and Canada to describe our awareness or lack of awareness to the reality of racial prejudice and institutional racism. There are secular and religious organizations, individuals, and denominations fighting for racial equality. But here is the question I would like to propose: Are we gaining greater understanding and greater acceptance or are we more confused and more powerless?

While you ponder an answer to this question, I would like to guide you on a journey to experience being compassionately integrated with individuals of differing ethnic and racial make-ups and perhaps even various socioeconomic levels coming together for the purpose of learning how to develop intentional multiracial friendships—perhaps a retreat setting or at a friend's home or even a church. Let's create an environment intentionally set to be a safe place where the Spirit of God anoints all those present through dialogue, fellowship, and worship. Imagine within this safe environment a place to process the fears and feelings of helplessness that penetrate our hearts when we face issues of race. Imagine a covenant of Christian believers joining together for the "soul" purpose of finding unity in the midst of indifference. Envision being nestled away in a beautiful corner of God's earth with friends and new friends, discovering the power of love, acceptance, honesty, humility, confession, forgiveness, and restoration, blessed with good food, fellowship, and worship. This is what motivates me. This is why I am persistent, persevering, and present in the church.

I live to encourage and empower believers in Christ to become equipped to fight "the good fight" for racial equality while standing firm on biblical truth with a focus on the cross. Ephesians 2:14–15 proclaims that Christ is our peace and multiracial worship consultant, in the hope that I can assist the church in exploring, creating, and sustaining multiracial congregations.

In case you are still pondering that question: Are we gaining greater understanding and greater acceptance or are we more confused and more powerless? I would like to offer a response that continues to move me towards greater understanding and acceptance. I refuse to be confused and in Christ! I am filled with Holy Spirit power!

Last year after reading one of Dr. Hollies' weekly columns in the *Grand Rapids' Times,* I knew that I had to respond to her question of "Why I embrace the Christian Reformed Church of North America." In 1996, the CRC's Ministry of Race Relations was mandated by its synod (denominational leadership) to design, organize, and implement programs that would assist the denomination's churches and members in eliminating the causes and effects of racism within the body of believers and throughout the world. Of course, this is a huge undertaking. But this written mandate affirmed my belief that my being created African American had great purpose.

One formative lesson I learned during my four years in seminary was that I do not have to stop being African American in order to be Reformed. I am called to this Dutch denomination because I am African American.

Anthony Carter, author of *On Being Black and Reformed* (Phillipsburg, N.J.: P&R Publishing, 2003) clearly gives definition to my calling as an ordained minister of the Word in the Christian Reformed Church. I join with him in saying:

> My white brothers and sisters need to know that most African Americans struggle with maintaining their cultural distinctiveness while embracing the truths of Reformed theology. My ethnic brothers and sisters need to know that this is not a white man's religion and that I am not leaving them behind but instead clearing a path on which we are to walk. My embracing the truths of the Reformation has become a stepping stone rather than a stumbling block.

While reading Carter's book I found that reformed theology aligns with the biblical, historical, and experiential accents of the African American church. I began my spiritual journey in a black Baptist church where the Bible was taught as final truth. I have found this same authority in Reformed theology. As well, both Reformed theology and the African American church remember and honor those who have gone before. My seminary training has taught me that history is vitally important in the acceptance of biblical truth. As a Bible believing Christian I was taught to practice what I believed. Reformed doctrines are experiential in that they preach life into the human experience. As I came to develop a reformed perspective on life it was evident that the sovereign plan and purpose of God was the same as I had come to know in the Baptist faith. I serve an Almighty God and truth is truth.

Yes I can be Reformed and African American. In the Gospel of Mark Jesus declared, "Is it not written, my house shall be called a house of prayer for all nations?" (Mark 11:17 NIV). Jesus was a multiracial preacher! Christians are called to be ambassadors of reconciliation. Reconciliation can only happen when peoples labor and live together. Time spent together, meals shared, senses of humor discovered, sensitivities explored—these things both require and build togetherness and reconciliation. Racial reconciliation is our future in heaven. We might as well get a head start.

This past year I was the first African American female to graduate from Calvin Theological Seminary in Grand Rapids, Michigan. In October, I was ordained to Word and Sacrament at the Church of the Servant Christian Reformed Church. Dr. Hollies participated in my ordination and gave clarity to this congregation about the giant step that all of us had taken to reach this point in history. I am encouraged to continue my journey with the people of God calling for integration. It is not yet clear to me how God will further guide my steps; however, I'm so encouraged by all of the women who have been sages to my life and ministry and offered me their counsel and experience. I have many miles to go before I can claim completion of the ministry God has set before me. We each have much work to accomplish to make this a reality for God. I'm so very appreciative of the support systems that surround me. And, now, I speak a word of persistence, perseverance, and being present to all of the people of God, in all of the places that we minister into each of our lives from this day and forever more. Please keep me and the sisters in this volume within your prayers, as we are praying for you. God has called us and I am truly . . . on the journey with ya!

~ BIBLIOGRAPHY

Essex, Barbara J. *Bad Girls of the Bible: Exploring Women of Questionable Virtue.* Cleveland: Pilgrim Press, 1999.

Grant, Jacquelyn. *White Women's Christ and Black Women's Jesus: Feminist Christology and Womanist Response.* Atlanta: Scholars Press, 1989.

Hollies, Linda H. *Bodacious Womanist Wisdom.* Cleveland: Pilgrim Press, 2003.

Jones, Charisse, and Kumea Shorter-Gooden, *Shifting: The Double Lives of Black Women in America.* New York: Perennial Press, 2003.

McKenna, Megan. *Rites of Justice: The Sacraments and Liturgy as Ethical Imperatives.* Maryknoll, N.Y.: Orbis Books, 1997.

McNeil, Brenda Salter, and Rick Richardson. *The Heart of Racial Justice.* Downers Grove, Ill.: InterVarsity Press, 2004.

Patterson, Sheron. *Put on Your Crown: The Black Woman's Guide to Living Single . . . and Christian.* Cleveland: Pilgrim Press, 2006.

Richardson, Brenda Lane, and Brenda Wade. *What Mama Couldn't Tell Us about Love: Healing the Emotional Legacy of Racism by Celebrating Oour Light.* New York: HarperCollins, 1999.

Robinson, Lori. *I Will Survive.* New York: Seal Press, 2002.

Shamana, Beverly J. *Seeing in the Dark: A Vision of Creativity and Spirituality.* Nashville: Abingdon Press, 2001.

Speller, Julia. *Walkin' the Talk: Keeping Africentric Faith and Culture in African American Congregations.* Cleveland: Pilgrim Press, 2005.

Townsend Gilkes, Cheryl. *If It Wasn't for the Woman.* Maryknoll, N.Y.: Orbis Books, 2001.

Watts, Deborah A. *101 Ways to Know You're Black in Corporate America.* Plymouth: Watts Five Productions, 1998.

Weems, Renita. *Listening for God: A Minister's Journey through Silence and Doubt.* New York: Simon & Schuster, 1999.

_____ . *What Matters Most: Ten Living Lessons in Living Passionately From the Song of Solomon.* West Bloomfield: Walk Worthy Press, 2004

Wimberly, Anne Streaty. *Soul Stories: African American Christian Education.* Nashville: Abingdon Press, 1994.

Wyatt, Gail Elizabeth. *Stolen Women: Reclaiming Our Sexuality, Taking Back Our Lives.* New York: John Wiley & Sons, 1997.

~ CONTRIBUTORS

Linda Boston, an ordained minister in the Evangelical Lutheran Church of America, holds a Doctor of Divinity degree from United Theological Seminary in Dayton, Ohio. She received her Master of Divinity from the Pacific School of Religion in Berkeley, California.

Gina Casey is an ordained minister in the AME Zion church. She is pastor of Fisher Chapel AME Zion Church in Phoenix, Arizona. She received a Bachelor of Business Administration degree from Howard University, Master of Science degree from American University in Washington, D.C., and a Master of Arts degree in theology and biblical studies from Fuller Theological Seminary.

Veneese V. Chandler is a member of Bethel Pentecostal Church Abundant Life Center Pentecostal Assemblies of the World (PAW). She is the executive director/CEO of Family Outreach Center in Grand Rapids, Michigan. She received her Bachelor of Science degree in psychology and her master's degree in education from Illinois State University.

Essie Clark-George is senior pastor of Israel CME Church in Gary, Indiana. She did her undergraduate studies at Northeastern University and received her Master of Divinity and Doctor of Ministry degrees from the McCormick Theological Seminary in Chicago, Illinois.

Sharon Ellis Davis is senior pastor of God Can Ministries, United Church of Christ, in Ford City, Illinois. She is also adjunct professor, McCormick Theological Seminary. She received her Master of Divinity degree from Chicago Theological Seminary, her Doctor of Ministry degree from McCormick Theological Seminary, and Ph.D. from the Chicago Theological Seminary.

Linda H. Hollies was senior pastor of Calvary United Methodist Church in Jackson, Michigan. She was a prolific writer and best-selling author. She also founded WomanSpace, Inc.

Lucille Jackson is co-pastor of James Memorial AME Church in Maywood, Illinois.

Michelle R. Loyd-Paige is a tenured sociologist at Calvin College in Grand Rapids, Michigan. She received her Bachelor of Arts degree from Calvin College, her Master of Science and doctoral degree from Purdue University. She is also the founder of Preach Sista! Inc.

M. Frances Manning is pastor of New Hope Baptist Church in Hackensack, New Jersey. She received her Bachelor of Arts degree from College of New Rochelle and her Master of Divinity and Doctor of Divinity degrees from New York Theological Seminary.

La Sandra Joyce Marie Melton-Dolberry is the founder, director, and pastor of Harambee Urban Ministries, a nondenominational ministry in San Diego, California. She attended the New Covenant Bible College and Center for Urban Ministries in San Diego.

Florida T. Morehead is senior pastor of the Shalom Ministries Christian Center in Fort Washington, Maryland. She holds an Bachelor of Science degree and a Master of Science degree in chemistry from the University of Arkansas, a Master of Divinity degree from Howard University School of Divinity and a Doctor of Ministry degree from National Bible College and Seminary.

Angela Taylor Perry is the minister of racial reconciliation at the Church of the Servant in Grand Rapids, Michigan. She received her Master of Divinity degree from Calvin Theological Seminary.

Paulette Sankofa is dean at the Christian Theological Seminary, Indianapolis, Indiana. She received her Master of Divinity from Eden Seminary and Ph.D. from St. Kate's University in Minnesota.

Patricia Spearman received her Master of Divinity degree from the Episcopal Theological Seminary of the Southwest. She is a retired lieutenant colonel in the United States Marine Corps and is currently a pastor in Las Vegas.

Daisybelle Thomas-Quinney is senior pastor of Wetumpka Church of God in Wetumpka, Alabama. She received her Bachelor of Science degree from Stillman College and the Master of Divinity degree from Pittsburgh Theological Seminary.

Joyce E. Wallace is a graduate of St. Paul's Seminary in Kansas City, Missouri, and pastor of Hardy United Methodist Church in Howell, Michigan.